VOLUME I OF THE PREVIOUSLY
UNCOLLECTED WRITINGS OF

GERTRUDE STEIN

REFLECTION ON
THE ATOMIC BOMB

edited by

ROBERT BARTLETT HAAS

*818
52
STEIN*

1973
BLACK SPARROW PRESS
Los Angeles

LIBRARY OF CONGRESS CATALOGING IN PUBLICATION DATA

Stein, Gertrude, 1874-1946.
    Reflection on the atomic bomb.

    (The previously uncollected writings of Gertrude Stein, v. 1)
    I. Title. II. Series: Stein, Gertrude, 1874-1946. The previously
uncollected writings of Gertrude Stein, v. 1.
PS3537.T323A6 1973 vol. 1   818'.5'209   73-13730
ISBN 0-87685-166-9
ISBN 0-87685-167-7 (pbk.)

TABLE OF CONTENTS

PREFACE: A Space Of Time Filled With Moving VII

I.   DIRECT DESCRIPTION

Wear (1914) 15
How Could They Marry Her? (1915) 16
Water Pipe (1916) 31
Relief Work In France (1917) 34
The Great American Army (1917) 36
One Has Not Lost One's Marguerite (1918) 37
J. R. (1919) 38
J. R. II (1919) 38
The Meaning Of The Bird (1919) 39
A Deserter (1919) 40

II.   PORTRAITS AND APPRECIATIONS

Mrs. Th——y (1913) 43
Mrs. Emerson (1914) 44
J. H. Jane Heap (1928) 49
An Indian Boy (1923) 50
A Stitch in time saves nine. Birds of a feather
  flock together. Chickens come home to roost. (1925) 52
Troubadour (1925) 53
Oscar Wilde Discovers America (1926) 54
Sir Francis Rose (1932) 56
Sir Francis Rose (1934) 56
Steiglitz (1934) 57
Picabia (1934) 58
Elie Lascaux (1935) 59
Sir Francis Rose (1939) 60
Sherwood's Sweetness (1941) 61
From Dark to Day (1945) 62
Raoul Dufy (1946) 63

III.   NATURE AND THE EMOTIONS

Vacation in Brittany (1920) 77
Ireland (1920) 79
Dinner (1921) 80
Readings (1921) 81

Today We Have a Vacation (1921) 82
Mildred's Thoughts (1922) 83
If He Thinks: A Novelette of Desertion (1922) 85
Procession (1923) 89

IV. PLAYS

Daniel Webster. Eighteen in America: A Play (1937) 95
Lucretia Borgia. A Play (1938) 118

V. LITERARY MUSIC

Studies in Conversation (1923) 124
Are There Arithmetics (1923) 127
Made A Mile Away (1924) 130
Descriptions of Literature (1924) 139
Five Words In A Line (1929) 142

VI. SYNTAX AND ELUCIDATION

We Came. A History (1930) 148
Evidence (1930) 153
Left to Right (1931) 155
Thoughts On An American Contemporary Feeling (1931) .. 159
Reflection on the Atomic Bomb (1946) 161

Sources and Acknowledgements 163

The dating of the above works is in all cases the date of composition rather than the date of periodical publication and follows the chronology established by Richard Bridgman in his *Gertrude Stein in Pieces*, Oxford University Press, 1970.

The portrait of Gertrude Stein on the cover of this book is taken from an oil by Pierre Tal-Coat painted in France in 1935. This oil is currently in the collection of Galerie Henri-Bénézit, Paris, and is reproduced with their kind permission.

Preface

GERTRUDE STEIN'S
"SPACE OF TIME FILLED WITH MOVING"

In the *Primer for the Gradual Understanding of Gertrude Stein* (1971) I tried to provide readers with "carefully chosen samples of each of the major periods of Gertrude Stein's writing, along with examples of each emerging or recurring style." That the volume has served its purpose by creating a new audience for Gertrude Stein has been made gratifyingly clear by the positive response of both readers and reviewers.

The purpose of presenting the Previously Uncollected Writings of Gertrude Stein is somewhat different: to make available again, and in one place (on the eve of her Centennial Year) the last large body of Gertrude Stein's writing to remain inaccessible because of its earlier appearance in obscure or transient periodicals.

Readers of the *Primer* will recognize that by 1914, the date of the first work in this anthology, Gertrude Stein had already passed through the two heroic shifts of style which determined her unique contribution to twentieth century American literature. The first involved a shift away from the chronological story line of traditional literature and a movement towards the moment-to-moment internal narrative voice of the writer. This move was a result of Gertrude Stein's recognition that her own subjective responses were a part of the "total situation" to be described. The second shift involved a movement away from seeing the world as a static universe and a shift towards seeing it as a world-in-progress. This move was the result of Gertrude Stein's acquaintance with the work and personality of William James.

Most of Gertrude Stein's literary innovations, beginning with *Things as They Are* (1903) and culminating in *Tender Buttons* (1910-1912) may be understood as new ways of abstracting—the playing out of the literary consequences of these two new ways of looking at things.

As I have written elsewhere, it was Gertrude Stein who first saw the æsthetic implications of James's pragmatic philosophy. Thus the vivid texture of *the present* became her "content", and the *pro-*

longed or *continuous present* became her compositional device. The structure of her language was intended to correspond to the structure of the dynamic events she was describing. In this way she felt she could give expression to what she considered the character of her own epoch: "a space of time filled with moving."

Variations on this theme are to be found in the various subsections of both the *Primer* and in these two volumes of Previously Uncollected Writings.

With the appearance of these texts in *Reflection on the Atomic Bomb* and the forthcoming second volume *How Writing Is Written,* the complete published writings of Gertrude Stein (in English) are at last available. That this should occur on the advent of her Centennial Year seems eminently right and a continuing evidence of Gertrude Stein's vital place in American Literature.

Robert Bartlett Haas
University of California
Los Angeles, 1973

REFLECTION ON THE ATOMIC BOMB
Volume One
Of the Previously Uncollected Writings of
GERTRUDE STEIN

I

Direct Description

Gertrude Stein found a new imagery in her description of the present. *This is nowhere more apparent than in the series of World War I poems which make up this section of the anthology. They were written "on location" in war-time France between the years 1914 and 1918. The situations described are the domestic or public events, kaleidoscopically seen, of a period of rapid change, social upheaval and fast crumbling tradition.*

In "Wear" Gertrude Stein demonstrates the subtle difference between repetition and insistence, the subtle sea-changes of sight, sound and sense freed from the pressure of conveying illustrative or narrative effects in language. The first paragraph is a grand bravura improvisation of "if" clauses finally coming to rest in a consoling declaration. The balance of the work is a series of declarative gestures made through the medium of an "I", a "she", a "he", and an "it". The conclusion, "All particulars", reminds us that the poem was a literal translation, in words, of things seen, heard and felt in successive moments of experience. Without resort to formal logic or literary convention, the author catches and expresses the essential tension and release of a total experience in her choosing and using of words.

"How Could They Marry Her" carries forward the mode of reliance on the back and forth movement of things heard: the question and answer, the statement and response of conversation. Traditional "meaning" is foresworn in favor of the new reaches of significance released through the play of simple words falling into unexpected relationships: "One cannot be independent if one has not got a comfortable chair." "Ardent fishes." There is play with both phrasing and punctuation: "Harry is all well. Harry is all well Harry is. All well." There are grandiose lists beginning with "I" or "we" or "why", or sometimes with lively participles. For the most part there are clear, clean, simple sentences. Gertrude Stein is vocalizing with her inner voice.

"Water Pipe" begins with a letter read aloud. It has all the earmarks of domestic chit-chat. Some sentences are too intense for the delay of internal punctuation: "Oh yes you are always inexact oh

yes you are." Or, "Yes yes yes." Embroidery, orchids, rooms, roses, tubs and water pipes, pansies, rain, dogs and doors give us the telling parameters of a bucolic landscape.

"Relief Work in France" is a suite of poems based on encounters with French soldiers and American doughboys in wartime France. When it appeared in Life, January 1917, entirely set in uppercase type, the anxious and inaccurate editor appended the following: "Miss Gertrude Stein sends us this contribution from Paris, and it has been set in the style of type in which Miss Stein's verses usually appear."

"The Great American Army" presents more war poetry in a vigorous, conversational style. It was printed with the following note in the June 1918 issue of Vanity Fair: "Gertrude Stein, the first and most representative of the so-called Cubists in prose, has, since the outbreak of the war, been living in France and working in war relief as an ambulance driver. Few American women have taken a more active part in the conflict than she. During the past few weeks, the continued arrival of our troops in France has inspired her to compose this poem." A patriotic flourish.

"One Has Not Lost One's Marguerite," published in Black and Blue Jay for April 1926, was thought by the editor to have entirely too much sequence. "I see already," he wrote, "that there is too much sense in this nothingness." Wartime loss, wartime consolation: "My poor Paul you are not intended for happiness in marriage. I fear so." Too much sense in nothingness.

"J.R.," "J.R.II," "The Meaning of the Bird" and "A Deserter" complete the long-uncollected war series, more of which may be found in Gertrude Stein's two books, Useful Knowledge and Bee Time Vine. They appear to be wartime portraits in direct description. When they were printed in Vanity Fair in March 1919 the editor's comment was: "Whether or not you like her art form—or lack of it, rather, whether or not you understand the cryptic meaning of her verses, there she is, and there is her influence, and there are her changes, and there they will remain."

One of the changes which should have been clear was that in

13

Gertrude Stein's writing the new notion of content required a new notion of form: the infinitely varied form was an extension of the infinitely varied moment-to-moment content. For Gertrude Stein the discipline was to make the form follow the function with exactitude.

It was to be a long time before even those who had begun to accept the changes in the form and content of the visual arts would accept these same changes in writing. In the meantime Gertrude Stein went right on using the present moment as the filter for selecting out the compelling elements of her environment. She went right on composing written works out of these snatches of direct description. The sparkling innovations of this period form her most characteristic and personal style.

WEAR

No not that and peculiarly, if you push the reason of being middle sized into the extreme little piece and you select actual endeavor, if you select actual endeavor, if you select, actual endeavor, the notion of religion, the notion of religion and peculiarly notice and peculiarly notice restless walk, if you peculiarly notice restless walk, if you peculiarly notice restless walk waiting, if you sanction meaning, if you represent recognized meadow pieces, if you furnish kites and horses, if you regulate traffic, if you mention other causes, all this does prejudice one against responsibility and lectures, and lessons, it further notices mistakes.

Poisons, Poisons are the means, minds are the means, old suns are the means, besides are the means. It is nugatory.

Fishes. Fishes are the means.

Did the war make you dash right in.

Or series. I did not guess why the expected elongated angle made a particular shadow speck. I expect it did.

I asked them about wash. They said washing. I cannot think that we can be unauthorized.

She went away and said that if I would not ask why there was a weeding of plain little pulled dahlias, she would not offer to cook.

He used to borrow a bicycle.

It isn't of much account anyhow. It was an enormous injustice. Excellent specimen. Reasonable readiness. All particulars.

1914

HOW COULD THEY MARRY HER?

I know what I want to do. I want to repeat all well.

By luck.

I pleased.

How could they.

I want to repeat or all well.

By good luck I married her.

I want to repeat is. I want to repeat is all. I want to repeat or is all. I want to repeat is all or is.

This is wrong.

It was genuinely tearful.

I wonder if I can do it.

He then said intending to spare that piece. Was it in order. It is difficult to telephone. We were accused of that. Not by them. I mean to be awful. Applause. We saw her then. I am sorry I spoke as if I were not pleased. It is too bad when she has that as a trouble and it is not necessary. She always brings it. Why should we have asked.

It is difficult to marry her. Not for him, certainly not after he was taught about Swiss swimming. He had been carefully so.

She was not poisoned.

Why are you hesitating.

I am doing something I have always wanted to do.

Is it fair to be sorry about it.

The plains which are filled with pleasure and distraction make one incline to obey when it is told to one that lights are needed for the evening. The whole evening is spent in invention.

I was so surprised.

This is my deception.

When I wished to acquaint myself with the reverie which would lead to the buying of horses and dogs I was not unacquainted with secrecy. This I showed by writing, by the way. This meant pleading.

Acquaintance with that method was authorized by the very painful scene that I had witnessed when I made a mistake. A mistake in dash. Clouds.

Reasonable clouds.

Clouds warranted that likeness.

I do not share that care.

CHAPTER I.

In a minute.

I was glad.

I was glad to be here.

I do not mind.

I do not mind the law. This is to say that I obey.

It begins to please. I play after noon. Late.

It begins to please me.

I wrote that I had heard that the flowers were shown. They were pushing their way. I said also that I did not, that it did not matter. That I was glad that she was better. That we all felt that. That it is irregular. What. Serbia.

Don't be mistaken.

When I count less I make mistakes.

Resolution.

I resolve to mend letters.

We had a pledge.

She was surprised. She did not expect that they would have ten thousand francs as yet. She was surprised. She was willing.

Why was she willing.

She wept they say.

I don't believe it.

I don't believe that.

I believe in saying Harry is all well. Harry is all well. Harry is all well. Harry is all well Harry is. All well. I believe in saying Harry is all well. By this I mean that I believe in Serbia. This is too astonishing.

Gradually there was melting. Of what. Of snow. Not to be wished for.

By that time everybody was distinguished.

By and by.

I don't say idling.

By ugly teasing.

Very ugly calling.

Very regular service.

By this time.

Now then.

We hated everything.

We were beside that perfect.

We were reasonable.

We were harsh.

17

We were neglectful.
We were persuaded.
We were tender.
We were tender.
We were resentful.
We were comfortable.
We were very fairly curious.

Then there was this question. Would we go if everybody went. Would we stay here or would we be equal. We would be wetter. We would equally be wondering. All of this made us clearly state that we wished to be strange. We were able to place relatives and this was rational. Any one could say that there was vengeance.

By this word.
Not at all.
Not easily.
Not beside difficulties.
Not by difficulty.
Not with difficulty.

By that noise. By really that noise. I don't see it. I do not see it. I do not care to see it.

When she came she asked if she might realise what it was to be boastful. She handled it tenderly.

By that time everybody was pleading.
I do not do.
Nobody respects money.
I really plead.
Pray for me.
Exactly questioned.
I spread glasses.
This is to see.

By all means many make claims. Many have claims. Many are originally wise. Very many are peculiar. Very many have babies. Very many wash something. Very many wear all their clothes negligently. Very many are accustomed to a costume. Very many are particular about the order of dissipation. They prefer boiled mutton and really there is not much of deceiving them.

Very many wear stockings that are beside all knitted. Very many do do these things. Very many are frequently annoyed.

It was so strange to win.
Everybody won.
It was nearly customary.

By noon a great many were grateful. I can understand it.

By original questioning and by maintaining silence the prints distinguished themselves. They were readily seen. All causes. All are causes. All scenes are followed. Then there was an exclamation. Lanquid lights are beneath contempt. I believe in union for liberty.

We are separated by ten times. They met and they were thankful. They meant to explain that and they were so searching in their glances that nobody was pale.

Authority.

What is happening.

Not really that any more.

Not by this means.

I am able to be gracious.

Please me.

Call me.

Have it.

Sea lion.

I do not mean to say another.

CHAPTER II.

Declare it.

Realise it.

Profane it.

Cæsar kisses. This makes a radiator. All the heat glows. Man furnishes 14 splendid examples. The rest is mainly established by relative insight into many ways of fishing. I fish for towns. Believing it. Remaining tall. Have that for care. Teasing many all are ably when they can able to wash babies. Washing stockings is more a reliance. A reliance to whom, to many kings.

Flies.

This is so far not reaching.

Plenty of us are mentioned.

CHAPTER III.

Begin again.

When a king said summer and another said not. When three kings were mentioned. When many were aroused by glances. I don't mean to-day. They were beneath snow. It sounded like it. I do not have to imagine anything.

There is no resemblance.

How do you like your two per cent.

CHAPTER III.

That's the way you know it's a play.

Please excuse me I meant to bring it in. I was selfish. I did mean to explain how I quarrelled. I quarrelled by asking her to be steadfast and earnest and stiff and resigned. I asked her to please anybody. I could not marry but I could be selfish. I really could be selfish. I could be earnest about it. I could go to Serbia.

Why do I mention that again.

Pleading. What is pleading. I don't make a mistake. All this was said in a hurry.

When they came in they were selfish.

There is no question about it.

We are not interested in the study of character.

Believing in Mrs. Thebes.

Believing in Mrs. Thebes I am not underrating any age or any garment or any such attraction. Believing in Mrs. Thebes I am believing in unmerited suffering.

This is wherein every one is incapable of expressing anything. By this I mean mentioning everything.

She came she said certainly.

I am writing.

I am sentimentally laughing.

I am curing all the time I am curing something.

I want to go.

By this I mean to be understood.

I do not wish simply to install myself. I wish to go too. We have the same ideas. That is the reason we agree. If we don't come he will not stay.

He asked for wounded scholars.

I was beside myself.

I have watched every day.

One cannot be independent if one has not got a comfortable chair.

This is obliged to be understood and all persons are exactly like a benediction.

We went.

We were early.

We were able.

We had strips of pleasant cakes. We were nearly vanquished. We had loud elephants. We were torn. We were reliable. We were able to go about. We were nearly worn out by it and we were patient. We were really patient.

I cannot forget to mention creeping.

I do not wish to go.

I am satisfied with telegraphing.

I feel that it is right to get advice.

I am peculiar.

I am peculiarly reluctant to have that made as a mistake. I do not wish to have it necessarily tacked on to a mere unit.

We were not covered.

How can I see that she is married. Any one can see something. By betraying what I know am I outraging any confidential undertone and is there really any reason why I shouldn't. I shouldn't be talkative. I should not have offered to do it. I should have been determined. I should be eager. By this means I can come to understand believing in all pleasures.

This is the story.

Among famous bottles and little roses and really there were no parties, in red and yellow which is painting when it is for a wagon with all this and special training it is not astonishing that each one was relaxed. Relaxed by indifference, relaxed by persuasion. Not relaxed by fortitude. Never painful, never really perfect, never arousd by a problem. The problem was is it at all violent, is it by that exceptional reason a persuasion. I can not help figuring.

By almost all colours he married again. Anybody is between difficulties and then where is it if we are all the children of one another. It is not strange that they are mountainous. They aren't when you come to think of it. Nearly everybody is ready. I don't want to hear them again. I don't know whom she married. I don't care to know too much about it because in that case I will have finished being a representative case.

By this time I was disgusted, I said if you are going to Serbia why don't you go. Why do you say you are going if you are not going. Why are you living a life of suffering. Why do you mislead not only yourself but many more, why don't you say earnestly I am not going. Why don't you ask your cousin. Why don't you suspect everybody, why don't you minister to a mind diseased, why are you careful, why are you capable of undertaking having two women, why do you delight in matches, why are you pressed to remain at home, in short, why don't you decide that you don't want to go.

This happened one day when Emily went out to pray. What did she pray for. She prayed that she might become more worthy of receiving an ecclesiastical education and that her address would become famous. She also prayed that there might come to be order and method in everything. She was apt to be refused by those English whom she had come to question. She was apt to be frightened by those hospitable friends who would not be pacified. She was certainly apt to be nervous. This is not a description of Emily.

By announcing millions she was readily perfect. By announcing many who came in she was left to independence. You cannot be independent if you haven't a chair. There is no use in reflecting on circumstances. When ideals are questioned there is no change in religion. By this means we all suffer.

Emily said new sin. She said it was questioning. She questioned nothing. She was religious and surviving. She meant to make more noise than anything.

You have brothers.

A busy life. I hoped to escape that. I think it is obliging.

A busy life.

They wear glasses.

Humming.

I expected her to meet me.

The principal reason for having a husband is that he looks like the King. I am very proud of him and he said he had delicate feeling. He was surprised that the daughter was not a married woman. He was surprised that she had an affair with anyone. When they came to see him, my husband I mean, they could not resist asking for everything. I can tell you.

I am so tired of vegetables. I said that if they would not put down my name I wouldn't care the least bit.

It is funny, isn't it, just wishing for puzzling, just wishing for wakening, just wishing for that before everything. All kinds of climates have that peculiarity.

What is conversation.

Any one can mention that. They can like kinds of pearls and old cakes and any old fashioned Italian. They can just see that way. I like Chinamen when they are European.

Imagine.

Imagine being one.

Imagine any kind of a chair.
My whole life is passed that way.

CHAPTER IV.

It is remarkable that in an especial assignment two lots were divided. One with the reasoning faculty and one without. This meant that they were all obliged to bow when they were together. They were not so very likely to be noticed. Not really more likely than their friends. They were measured and indeed many people had it nevertheless clearly that certain simplicity is contemplated. They were not surprising. We thought they were. We thought every one of them had some way of eliminating organisation and really it would not be careless, it was by any such stroke that they made mountains. They were either original or merely mercenary. If you were rich what would you do. You would spend money. How would you spend money. By being pale.

Anyway they smiled.

I don't seem to be interested in whether they have ambiguity. I don't doubt that they are not objecting to reflections. They seem to be obligatory. They have healthy hands. They are so sober.

When I join pale ties with white top shoes and really splendid treasure, I am not feeble, I am gregarious. I mean to stay at home.

It is not very likely that louder horses snort. They have fellow houses and little low shades. They make a thousand piles of pillows. They are each one of them earnest.

I am going certainly.

Please be seated.

What help will be given.

Help that is fanciful.

I do not wish to use the word fanciful.

CHAPTER V.

By the time everybody was perfect there was no father. By that time it was a shock. It had been their habit to go about in their motor car. They saw the futility of leading an independent life.

It is not tantalising to have a colour for the hair, it is not at all tantalising, when it has been explained. Take my hat off.

Do not be prepared to come.

They asked me about Spain. They asked me about a Spanish bed, they asked me about early customs. They asked me about their point of view. They asked me if I was inclined to agree. They asked me if I would prefer to bother. They asked me to be ready. They asked me why I was so cheerful. They did ask me about all the callers. They asked me to tell them about my life. They asked me if I ever knew any other way of traveling. They asked me if I was disappointed.

I can't describe a house. Beside that, he wouldn't give me a long lease. He said he was not certain if it would suit him. He said he felt inclined to try it. Anyway I decided to give up London.

The reason that I decided to give up London was that I once said that he would be suffering. How was he suffering. Dear, dear.

He did.

The climax was reached.

There was no hustling.

She was his friend.

As we heard the story it was true that she was his friend. She had her room and her graces and she would absolutely not wear jewelry. She was pained by resemblance.

When we met her we found that she did wear jewelry, that she had an emerald, that she admired combinations of stones and that she was really puzzled by flowers.

To be puzzled by flowers is an illusion.

If one talks quickly one knows one is not perfect.

By that time terms are made and a good memory, well, a good memory is mentioned three times.

I cannot tell a consecutive story. I am particularly pleased by ranges. We were going to have a white one.

Dining.

When you dine with me you must eat chestnuts. If not rice and more than that you can have anything you care to have. I am easily pleased by anyone insisting. It is so restless to have a cross moment. No one can decline enough. I don't say that to stare. I don't really say it on my birthday. I say it when I feel like it, that is to say, when I feel inclined to dress.

I should be ordered about and I wouldn't pause I wouldn't pause to carry away all the circumstances. I should fail to propose a settled refusal. This is so easily done by anyone. Any refusal is for an evening.

CHAPTER VI.

How could they.

We haven't seen her all week.

They even asked if she had gone to Serbia.

Please mention this that they even asked if she had gone to Serbia.

When we first heard the story we thought it was very different. We thought she had suffered because of coming in direct contact by means of a combination of being together with one who by reason of her nationality could not help evading retribution and realisation. This was a thing that went in so completely with what we were then feeling that it was perfectly astonishing to us. We had come to believe that each one met a merry one and that each one was a merry one and that each one voiced that merry one and so on, to laughing. We were pleased with the added illustration and we often quoted it. We were not mistaken. We had an omission. We had not fainted. How is it that we had not questioned it. Because we were so sure.

When we had been told everything it was not disconcerting. How could it be disconcerting if we were told everything. By nearly every one models were staring. They wear hats this year and by this time we have been told everything.

I made a mistake. I thought I wrote in the book, I thought I was writing in the book, I hadn't made a mistake.

She wants to go to Serbia. I can understand lots of ways of wishing to go to Serbia show resolution and courage and forethought.

I can understand perfectly well why she doesn't want to see me.

She found that different ways of saying, I will not go alone, were not expected from one another. They were always beside it. They were uneasy and beside that was it flourishing. It was flourishing, if you want to look at it that way.

How could they marry her.

Serbia. What is powder. Powder is liquid and in movement and a cousin a cousin is willing to sacrifice her.

What is a coward. A coward is anyone who is willing to go to Serbia. Who is willing to go to Serbia some one without a heart. I was cured of that.

Her hair turned there.

This afternoon when we were looking at her hand we found that the impression we had had was the one we stated. We found that it is not difficult to explain that. We found that there were words, parts of words, and letters, and we knew strength. Strength is wonderful.

She says she is equal to it.

We looked and when we saw what imagination meant, what separation meant, what politeness meant, we were no longer surprised that we had that impression.

They are two. They do not resemble each other. They are not tall and they change their clothes.

I would have been better pleased if there had been more bother.
Potatoes.

I remember potatoes.

I will not finish with that. I am more resolute than anyone would expect.

I am not going to be led about.

CHAPTER VII.

In this chapter I am going to tell about how nearly captivity is not surprising. It comes with war. Someone who was totally not expecting to have any change of arbitration suddenly finds conversation as he had suspected advancing. Someone suddenly finds conversation advancing to that point that makes it possible to ask do you believe in refinement, do you hesitate for a word. Do you say that that you have a particle of violence. Do you discern features. Do you mend fans. That is playful. Do you mend fans.

No we just chat.

Now then this isn't at all what she describes. Not at all. She says that he is in prison, that he has always been very delightful about everything about eating and everything and while it is shocking it is a pity and there is nothing stupid about offering what one can.

She doesn't really discern yet and yet her imagination, her imagination is decidedly crumbling not crumbling for hunts. Not at all shadowed. It was a pleasant surprise.

Etta said that she, meaning another, was not going.

She said she was not going.

She meant to be careful.

I don't believe there was any reason for it.

I forgot I was speaking about war.

CHAPTER VIII.

How could she.

I wish to find an experienced nurse to leave immediately with our party for where the Urgent Fund for Serbian wounded is establishing a base hospital under the Serbian Government. Should this mission appeal to a nurse in Paris I would be glad to have her call at my address, between ten and noon, or between three and five p.m.

I meant to put in that word. They went together. They went visiting. They stayed a minute. They did not refuse to stay. That was imaginable.

Long calling, hours of annoyance, pleasant phrases, bitten curls, really actual places and more than that, sombre fortunes, those together make anyone uneasy.

Could it be a mystery.

I ask you, could it be a mystery?

Yes.

It could be a mystery.

I wonder if I have made a mistake. Could I by any chance have been wrong about it. Could there have been no occasion for freely destroying prestige.

Dear one.

I announce this.

We will not come by water.

CHAPTER IX.

Boiling.

Ardent fishes.

I do wish I were unprincipled.

Boiling.

Ardent wishes.

I do wish I was left out. I do wish I was bewildered. I do wish I was told that I was a bookworm. Really I do. I wish I was likely to be left in it by that one. I wish I were peaceful. I have plenty of plans.

I have decided that I would rather he didn't.

Serbia.

What is it.

Why is it not annoying.

It is not annoying because arrangements have been made.
Serbia.
Why isn't it annoying.
Why is it not annoying.
It is not annoying because arrangements have been made.
Eleven. Eleven chapters.
I wonder why I listen.
I listen because I can see the handles which make doors creak.
What is a Spanish bed.
Go on.

Their plans were these. They intended to install a hospital.
Everybody knows about that. They intended not to leave it out. They
were resolute. They were determined and principled and they were
not aggressive nor were they boisterous. They were ready for an
exchange between them and between those. Thy were ready for the
purpose of devoting themselves to that country. After that they ex-
changed other ways. They sent word. They were wise and silent.

It is really astonishing that I don't care.
Easy going like a dying lady.
Is it a complex and fascinating form of art. I finished one and I
made another.
Did I say.
I came again and I thought they didn't want me.
I came again explaining.
Why do you wear hats.
It's a word I use.
Seeing her makes passion plain.
I hope to reach hers.

CHAPTER X.

This is the last chapter before ten.
This is the time which has come.
I am not deaf to reason.
We ask it of one another.
Politely crying.
Dear me.
I am going on not to swim but to be careful of who knows.
Who knows that.
I do.
Careless, yes it's careless to be brave.

I am brave.

I am not neglected by my father.

Please be so kind.

Please be as kind as you are. Please be kind.

A little reason for kindling.

It is a new form of wit.

Spots and dirt and would you be afraid of a mother.

Who could scare leaves. I. Surely not I.

She said she would not go.

She said I love her so.

Believe fools. Tell them that they get there first.

Be attentive. I am going on. She is going too.

Had you thought that she wasn't.

Did you think that she hadn't intended to be leaving.

Had you thought she hadn't been deciding.

Were you thinking that she hadn't been intending to be going.

Were you thinking that she wasn't going.

Have you been thinking that she hadn't intended being going.

Did you think she wasn't going.

Were you thinking that she wasn't intending going.

Mightn't you have been thinking that she hadn't been intending to go.

Hadn't you been thinking that she hadn't been intending to be going.

Had you been thinking that she didn't intend to be going.

Didn't you think she was going.

Were you thinking she wasn't going.

CHAPTER XI.

This is the last chapter. Chapter eleven.

This is the last chapter about going. This is the last chapter about going.

They came here. They said they had many applicants. They said they were stiff and riding. They said they were courteous. They said they were leaving. They said that beside that they were courteous and they said that they were deciding. They certainly were not miserable.

Lack of interest.

Lack of interest.

Alfred says I am all well. Come up. Come up.

Alfred says I am all well. Alfred says I am all well.
Alfred knows I am all well.
Pearls fall and that's all.
As if you weren't very methodical.
No Alfred.
As if it were not for that purpose.
In came you were supreme.

1915

WATER PIPE

I ask you to speak. I ask you to give directions every five minutes. I ask you if you think that it is splendid that photographs are copied in embroidery. I know what your answer will be. I do not mean to say that I can anticipate it. Believe me that I sign myself yours obediently.

Rose Bonnett.

Pleasures of prophecy. I said we would travel. You said certainly we will travel but not yet. The pleasure of prophecy.

We are of the same opinion concerning orchids. We do not prefer black ones but we find them more sombre.

You will give me orders will you not. You will tell me what you prefer. You will ask for what you want. You do need the door closed. Please do not mind if I refuse at first. I don't like to find out exactly where the draft comes from. But I see what you wish, you need to have instant obedience and you shall have it. I will never question. Your lightest wish shall be my law.

I have no objection to a signature. I sign with your pen. I say frequently I have asked that you write it for me.

To you I'll be true.

Yes that's it. Of course that's it. If you don't care to listen I am willing to read. Shall I read aloud.

I once made a description of a tub. A tub holds water, not drinking water. Water is for the tub. A tub is liable to cheese, not in this country, it can hold ducks yes it can hold ducks and others. Besides that fish is not necessary. We do not like such fish. A tub is perpendicular. Do be careful not to arrange it. I like to ask a question.

We can be reasonably careful.

I did forget to mention sugar.

Fine sugar.

There are lots of ways of arranging roses. We like ours white and red and pale color.

No one makes fun of me.

Oh yes you are always inexact oh yes you are.

Yes she is.

I know where I please. We will speak of it. A new mattress I

31

can't help. You can have it. You must have it. Dear. Dear.

Did you say water-pipe or water-pipes.

Yes yes rats.

Do you remember when we used to say rats.

If they use an envelope is it the same as a package.

Electricity has many uses.

That is a pretence.

No it was not rude. A great many people object to the electric light.

Thanks so much for the candle.

Yes Yes.

Yes pansies.

Kindness to many.

Yes Yes Yes.

I reminded you that it needed to be cleaned.

No you didn't remind me you told me.

Oh yes.

This is not your favorite. The water pipe is not your favorite. I understand your preference and yet we are singularly not deficient. I do not believe in mountains. I do believe in hills. We are surrounded by them. It is very healthful.

This is not interesting this isn't at all interesting.

Do you believe in victory.

I don't think much of oranges.

What is the name of it.

A little way to go.

Any little think makes a conversation. By that I do not mean I envy my neighbor and besides they don't use it.

Oh yes they do.

A great deal of it did you say.

A great deal of it.

Don't please me.

There is a fire next door.

Did she make it.

Of course some things are lost.

Water trickles.

And pansies. No fenel.

Water-pipes and pencils.

A little water-pipe. I have it here.

Of course you mean a water-pipe.

We watched and saw how they fixed it.

This was a very strange matter.

A little visiting and so speedily done.
Indeed water-pipe.
We said water was not lost.
It isn't.
Not nearly so much wind.
In conclusion I ask for water.
Are you not content with the rain.
I am very content with it.
Plenty. Why do the dogs like water.
It is very irregular.
You mean to say the little one.
Yes Yes.
A great deal of it did you say.
A little water-pipe. Call me. Water pipe a plan.
A little piece of it.
We will see to it.
I am very sorry that we are troubled.
No trouble.
There is never any danger.
Oh yes I understand that.
Naturally you do and now will you go in.
Into the house.
But we leave the door open.
Yes of course.

1916

RELIEF WORK IN FRANCE

THE ADVANCE

In coming to a village we ask them can they come to see us. We mean near enough to talk; and then we ask them how do we go there.

This is not fanciful.

MONDAY AND TUESDAY

In the meantime what can we do about wishes?
Wish the same.
Agreed for a minor.
And for my niece. What are you doing for my niece?
Baby clothes.
And milk.
Malted milk.

THE RIGHT SPIRIT

The right spirit. There are difficulties, and they must be met in the right spirit.

This is an illustration of the difficulties we have in many ways.

Then we go on.

VICTORY

Queen Victoria and Queen Victoria.
They made you jump.
And I said the mother; you said the mother. I did not remember the mother was in Paris, but you did.

AGAIN

When the camellias are finished the roses begin.
Are the French people healthy?
I think them healthy.
And as to their institutions?
As to their institutions. There is no doubt that they like a park.
And forests?
In the sense in which you mean, yes.
That is a question I meant to ask.
It is answered.

1917

THE GREAT AMERICAN ARMY

I found an acorn to-day.
Green
In the center.
No, on the end.
And what is the name of the bridge?
This is what we say.
"The Great American Army,"—
This is what we say.

I write to loan.
We do work so well.
And what must *we* do?

In the world.
What do you call them?
Plates.
And where do you use them?
In guns.
The French pronounce it Guns.
So do the English.
What do the boys say?
"*Can* we?"

In the middle.
Or in the middle.
The Great American Army.
Nestles in the middle.
We have hope;
Certainly—
And Success!

1917

ONE HAS NOT LOST ONE'S MARGUERITE

One cannot say one has lost one's Marguerite.
And then they went ahead of him. Not of him.
Of her. Not only of her.
Not of them.
One cannot say anything.
In that case let us smile.
Don't be too stout.
In a minute.
Can you consider dwelling.
Can you expect noises.
In the meantime let us wish for the van.
In asking then are we asking too much.
We are not.
We will be gratified.
My poor Paul you are not intended for happiness in marriage.
I fear so.

1918

J. R.

In the midst of it.
And the respected fields.
Did you have the pleasure of an American.
Indicated.
And then what happened.
Did you write to me.
Dearie me.

1919

J. R. II

In there.
Well naturally.
In there well naturally.
We had fish and Serbs and pleasure.
Well naturally.

1919

THE MEANING OF THE BIRD

To imitate a bird.
To play baseball.
To sing on a truck.
To have feather hair.
To be attended.
To belittle water.
To like ice.
To egg on girls.
And to wish to be paid.
And to buy shoes.
And to do that.
And to do that
Is Nimes
As she seems
With United Statiens
With feathers for tens
Of thousands
Who love ice creams
Alas there is none in Nimes.

1919

A DESERTER

Simple Narcissus flung in a flower.
It does sound like that.
Are you sorry for him.
Both brothers dead
That has nothing to do with it.
Colic and indeed he was sick.
That was from working.
Working by us.
Who then Narcissus in then the box.
Can you think this is funny.

I cannot forget Narcissus Deschamps. He was a deserter. He had had them brothers killed in the war. He was a professor and took pleasure in a bout of box. He told us he was an autombile assayer. He worked very well and he got the colic and the police caught him.
We know him.

1919

II

Portraits and Appreciations

One of Gertrude Stein's "great forms" is the portrait, *a literary genre which has a distinguished history reaching back to the earliest records glorifying kings and heroes.* The Greeks produced *"formal prose memorials" of patriots who fell in battle, individual portraits of ideal men.* The Romans produced "authorized lives." *Career, action or character were the emphasis.* Plutarch used de-*tails, dramatized incidents, anecdotes and generalizations to enliven his biographical sketches.* Suetonius added sex and scandal. Ger-*trude Stein used all this and more.*

After the medieval plethora of Saint's lives, the briefer literary portrait emerged: La Rochefoucauld and La Bruyère produced telling pictures of their contemporaries "combining psychological understanding and literary polish." These caractères *or* anatomies *have reached their peak in the* lives *of eminent Victorians and in the psychological* profiles *of the twentieth century.*

Gertrude Stein's multi-faceted portraits *bring a new flexibility to an old tradition.*

"Mrs. Th[ursb]y" and "Mrs. Emerson" date from the period of Gertrude Stein's literary cubism. Things were seen in the present— memories, resemblances and past associations were excluded by severe discipline and choosing. Note the Bessie-Bertha passage of "Mrs. Emerson." The immediate, the unique and the vivid in things seen, heard and felt were carefully included.

Portraits from the later periods may be found in Gertrude Stein's Geography *and* Plays *(1922),* Useful Knowledge *(1928), and* Portraits and Prayers *(1934).*

"An Indian Boy" and "Jane Heap" are portraits from Gertrude Stein's "Romantic" period. Full of play, gentleness and gardens.

The balance of the pieces in this section may be seen not only as portraits but as encomia. *No doubt these fugitive pieces were done rather spontaneously in response to a request for the review of a friend's book or for an introduction to a painter's catalogue. Those so honored, in various literary styles: Sherwood Anderson, Alfred Kreymborg, Lloyd Lewis, Sir Francis Rose, Alfred Steiglitz, Francis Picabia, Elie Lascaux, Pierre Balmain and Raoul Dufy.*

This rather sentimental support of her friends is quite consistent with Gertrude Stein's theory of criticism: "Nobody needs criticism, only appreciation."

Gertrude Stein's portraits and reviews were appreciations.

42

MRS. TH————Y

A landed break. The blown crane in a cane that is not personal, the only crest that is a criminal girdle, the absence of the blessed and the presence, the presence more, the presence, more. The presence in a praise and a very ugly lily, no uglier than silly, no uglier than a lily, a lily a round lily, a lily is no lily. A recent stretch of no backward breath makes it go farther further and further any further a line of settlings shine in all that is no bestower. No silence, no silence, and more stretch of no steepness curly, no curly, nothing in curly, nothing in white and grey and pink altogether. No blindness is actual in sight and sudden color and quality of chasing and mighty little expression. No breath is antagonistic and no sudden mouth which is closed makes any other wool entirely wood and paper, no other wood and wet places in a after all a serpent and a beggar awful in no cloth that is not cleaner and cleaner. A special rate of putting tumblers into tumble places and three languages more. A pressed egg glass is a pressure ever. A pressed egg glass is tremendous, it is ideal, it is irrevocable. It is hindooed it is declaimed, certainly declaimed necessarily in antagonism and unrest and a rising ringing, a rising and ringing, a rising, a rising rinsed with snow and no sun, no more sun hardly. The curly sedate example of no more than the height in topazes and if necessary no older amethysts, the curly ready collision with a single blame for hair and for the pinch of scissors and anything altogether, the curly center which is not connected with curls altogether singularly, shows the education, it does show pining, it does even show claret and gums articulately and in the meantime before and after. Nothing is more curious to a purpose.

1913

43

MRS. EMERSON

The regular way of instituting clerical resemblances and neglecting hazards and bespeaking combinations and heroically and heroically celebrating instances, the regular way of suffering extra challenges, the regular way of suffering extra changes, the regular way of suffering extra changes the regular way of submitting to exemplars in changes, the regular way of submitting to extraordinary celebrations, the certainty, because keep centre well half full whether it has that to close when in use, no not repeatedly, he has forgotten.

Now then.

Now then shining, now then shining.

Mrs. Evangeline Henderson went in. She said that the morning. She said that in listening. No I will not be funny.

Pleasing pleasing pleasing.

Little words frankly, your game is not a silly game. Birds are so restive.

Not that to-day to-night believe the corrected list believe more blotter than the red. I said I knew America.

My sister she is not my sister, my sister she is my sister her plan is to be represented by absolutely the same letter paper.

One day one day.

I cannot see I cannot see I cannot see. I cannot see.

I cannot see beside always.

I have not selected my pronunciation. I have not selected my pronunciation.

I will repeat I will not play windows. In the new houses there are not windows for ventilation or any other use. They say that that is their use. They say that kindly amazing lights they say that kindly amazing lights and they say no that is not the use of a word, they say that unkindly certain lights, anyhow when I am pronounced that certain cheerful shapes are fainter, they say that they have pronounced exceptionally.

The beginning of little winning the beginning of little winning claims. If you say little winning if you do not separate that is if you do not separate between, if you do not separate between if in in not in, all the pronunciations, all the pronunciations.

All the chances of intermediate investigation are so argued that the recent disturbances fit the first change in silent rugs. Silent rugs. I thought that I would state that I knew certainly that she was so seen that if her eyes were so placed not violently not verbally so placed. She is not agreeable. She is not so agreeable. I wish I could safely legitimise, and I will. I think it is what I said what I reorganised in mounting her. I mounted her there. Deliberate. She has a son not a son he was a thicker one. I go on. Begun.

Bessie is like Bertha.

I can see that if you did the reason would be that there was certainty.

If heating is beside the meal and the selection of masterpieces makes communication, communication is ardently rechosen, communication is suddenly respected, communication is suddenly resumed, communication is suddenly rested, communication is suddenly respected, communication is suddenly respected, communication is suddenly chosen communication is suddenly chosen.

No use, no use in resolving that Bertha is piled, no reason in slackening, that is a word, that is a word severely, of no do not deceive the more important asking if you have never been to a collection of repeated references.

I do not say that green is believed to be that colour. I do not say that green makes lips, I do not say that they colour stations, I do not say that she would spread it into I hope that I believe that I select that I retain. I hope that no occurence and no surprise and no concerning question. I do not wish to hear it again.

Oh well not now anyway. You do say it. Oh cannot you see that the price is allowed that the complete wrecking of louder sounds.

I cannot help it, Bessie is like Bertha, I see the resemblance I resolve to silence confusions I shall believe no pointed singularities I cannot see why a dog is black and a voice is necessary. I cannot see why a voice is necessary. Paula. Paula said that she would not care to see her again. Paula.

Bessie I do not wish to mention Bertha. I can simply explain that.

I do not wish to mention Bessie I can refer that.

I do not select to have similar sounds. Bertha can be surrounded. Bertha can be surrounded, Bertha can be surrounded by so much saliva. Peace to children.

When I state when I state and restate when I restate I say that there is a ceiling. A ceiling is a roof. A roof is formidable, formidably speaking, a roof is formidably speaking.

Now I turn away.

45

Please copy this. Others able to copy this. Others able to copy this after. After measure.

I have come to research. Bessie refers to Bertha not to Bertha. Bessie refers to Bertha.

I like hesitation. I like the pleasing selection of respectable shouting. I like recreation. I like surrounding dear papa.

More and more the original cause is forgotten. She wished to see her son-in-law. She met her daughter who was coming down from being depressing. She is of course everything. This is a mistake it is an early morning train.

When she met me she had much to tell.

We went out and were arriving. Scarcely pleasures. Scarcely pleasures extraordinarily. Scarcely pleasures slightly in advance of extreme kindness. Now that he is well and strong and knowing their extreme anxiety he was well and strong knowing her extreme anxiety.

Please direct that she is not to say that she is not say Bertha or Bessie. Please direct that she is not to say not Bertha. Please to direct.

Will you give this to your fathers.

It is natural without children natural.

Hesitating and certainly. Between that and pointing to his service later they make this. They didn't expect that Hannah would be in it. They didn't expect that he would seem to be sat upon a single piece of cardboard box.

It is very irresponsible to be a little neglected and then comes the question of pulling.

One of his brothers the man was descending by his brother. They thought nothing of it naturally one would have objected. They seemed searchful.

It gives you some arrangement you see.

No I don't think so.

He says that selfish selling is more likely than selfish bewildering.

I do not care to remember what I do not feather. I do not remember whether a flavour is farther. I do not remember whether cork tins are believed to be older. I do not care to mention any other.

I do not care to bewilder.

I do not care to sell her. I do not care to be a locked cellar. I do not care to be cheerier.

I say I do know Bessie. Bessie resembles Bertha. Paula resembles Bessie. Bessie resembles Bertha Bessie resembles Bertha. I do not offer to determine whether Paula and Bertha and Bessie are distinctly separate.

It is especially getting bigger. It is especially slighter. Why is there a change in water colour. Water is coloured by the sudden departure of all the interested readers of a newspaper.

I meant to say that it is necessary to spill all there is where there is and I say that I incline to believe that more that the more often I see it everywhere the more often. She'd be just lonesome which would show that the same water is not behind the mountains. I have heard it mentioned. I expect to get a recommendation and I will not say it is for suggestions.

You are down to nineteen.

The same.

How is Bessie this morning.

Please say a baby.

I do not leave the same all day and I do not share unless you are coming to caress country.

I do not like having said that I do not see why an excuse is preferable. I do not like the sound of spreading. I do not like the meaning of the late carpet. I do not believe in wretches. I do not like whispers. I do love to say such very hurried papers. I do mean to believe that soldiers order pearls. I do mean to say that it was a tumbler.

I am getting rather anxious.

Really I am getting rather anxious.

The way to show shapes is to realise to realise rightly that mentionings are abominable.

I can't help it I can't help hearing carrots.

I do help it, I do help it fastening chocolate.

A secret time in spinning.

Messes remembered mentioning. They remembered mentioning cleaning. They remembered mentioning, they saw eight angles, they meant to do mending.

This is a little climb in when.

Not to-day.

Yesterday, not some day.

Yesterday.

Wretched creature.

Wretched reason for winter. Really not at all.

I wish I had a certain rain.

Then a little barometer.

Then a dry cellar.
Then a dog which means to be old.
Then all the exceptional white.
Then a climbing bell.
Then more water.
Then all over it.
I wish I had to go and get her.

1914

J. H. JANE HEAP

FAIRLY WELL

An Appreciation of Jane

He seemed that anybody is all of that ordinary come from arrangement agate a gate and tree and she looks like Grace which is true. There are three of them that look like Grace Grace and Brake and many many used to be all gold used to be all gold where it is digging as a predeliction it is an elimination elevation partial periodic objection to pine trees selling call use it but theirs is that a plenty of cutting makes meals a suggestion of what and the evening she came in the evening and she stayed late and the morning she came and stayed late in the evening. She came and stayed late the first time in the evening in the morning she left to stay late in the morning. This is was just the first time. This all to say that Jane Heap any way did stay late the first time in the morning and the evening. She came in the evening and she stayed late and the morning she came and stayed late in the evening. How sweet it is and yet how bitter and it is might is right. She might be right. This is what there is to say to Jane Heap just at break of day in the morning. Jane Heap the first day stayed late in the evening. Fairly well is very good.

Jane Jane come away let the garden come and stay came late to stay in the morning came late to stay in the first day in the evening.

Margaret Anderson Margaret and Anderson, Jane whose is it. Whose is it when it is a name day. Whose is it when it is a name a day. Whose is it. Jane a day a Jane a day. Whose is it when a Jane a day a day a Jane add a Jane a day. Think a day a Jane a day. Think Jane a day. Think Jane think a day. A Jane a think a day. Think Jane a day. Think Jane a think a think a Jane a think a day. It was while she was away a think a Jane a day.

Jane it is however how had how it tried that it was J.H. or Jane Heap. Jane was her name and Jane her station and Jane her nation and Jane her situation. Thank you for thinking of how do you do how do you like your two percent. Thank you for thinking how do you do thank you Jane thank you too thank you for thinking thank you for thank you. Thank you how do you. Thank you Jane thank you how do you do.

1928

AN INDIAN BOY

It happens to be here.

Black and white and red all over.

One little Indian two little Indian three little Indian boys five little four little three little two little one little Indian boy.

They were all anxious to go. I accidentally met some one else. I said to him, where have you been. And he said I have been. And I said to him and what were your experiences. And he answered they do not understand the proper use of violets. Violets and mimosa, these can please.

Another instance of the thing I mean is this. They were in the midst of excitement and she was there and she was not representative. In this way no mistake can be made.

And an Indian boy.

Five Indians as we said we know how to say five Indians as we said. We are amused when we say who is abused as we say.

An Indian boy in Mexico.

An Indian boy in India.

An Indian boy in America.

An Indian Boy in Russia.

Also an Indian boy in Georgia.

An Indian boy in Italy.

An Indian boy in India.

An Indian boy in Africa.

An Indian boy in America.

An Indian boy and individuals and close answers.

She said a big fig and she said they had Jocelyn.

An Indian boy in India in America in Africa in Georgia in Italy and in Asia.

And an Indian boy and individuals and close answers.

AN INDIAN BOY.

An Indian boy was said to be red.

He leaves no doubt as to this.

An Indian boy is said to be red and he leaves no one in doubt of this.

An Indian boy says he is red and so no one has any doubt of this.

An Indian boy or is he red and is there any doubt of this.

If an Indian boy can naturally be an inhabitant is there any doubt of it.

An Indian boy being an inhabitant is there any doubt about it.

By naturally being an Indian boy and an inhabitant may one say that may be he is but we doubt it.

An explanation of the situation as to an Indian boy being an inhabitant leads to the expression of doubt of this on the part of these who do doubt this.

An Indian boy is an inhabitant of this place and he has no doubt about it.

Dawson Johnston Librarian. What is gentle. To gentle. To be gentle.

AN INDIAN BOY.

Can the first one see me.
Can the second one see me.
Can the third one see me.
Can the fifth one see me.
Can the fourth one see me.
Can the third one see me.
Can the second one see me.
Can the first one see me.

When I see them and they see me I say to them that I see them and that they see me.

An Indian boy can very nearly see to this. An Indian boy can very nearly come to see to this. An Indian boy can be very nearly said to have seen to this.

An Indian boy nearly an Indian boy and very nearly an Indian boy. When I say all this I remember that choice.

An Indian boy can say what to say.

And an Indian boy can say what does he say.

He says he needs to say he needs to be able to say what he can say.

An Indian boy can say what he says and he says that there is a singular relief in two daughters. A singular relief in two daughters. In their relief he was not disappointed.

When he sees he sees to it that they are celebrated to-day.

An Indian boy can be satisfied.

An Indian boy can be satisfied and by the outcropping of a central hill. He can be satisfied.

If you mean to be reconciled if you mean to be altogether reconciled can they say another may another may ask a question eight times and nine times.

1923

A STITCH IN TIME SAVES NINE. BIRDS OF A FEATHER FLOCK TOGETHER. CHICKENS COME HOME TO ROOST.

[Review of *A Story-teller's Story* by Sherwood Anderson.]

There are four men so far in American letters who have essential intelligence. They are Fenimore Cooper, William Dean Howells, Mark Twain and Sherwood Anderson. They do not reflect life or describe life or embroider life or photograph life, they express life and to express life takes essential intelligence. Whether to express life is the most interesting thing to do or the most important thing to do I do not know, but I do know that it is the most permanent thing to do.

Sherwood Anderson has been doing this thing from his beginning. The development of the quality of this doing has been one of steady development, steady development of his mind and character, steady development in the completion of this expression. The story-teller's story is like all long books uneven but there is no uncertainty in the fullness of its quality. In detail in the beginning and it does begin, in the beginning there is the complete expression of a game, the boys are and they feel they are and they have completely been and they completely are. I think no one can hesitate before the reality of the expression of the life of the Anderson boys. And then later, the living for and by clean linen and the being of the girl who has to have and to give what is needed is without any equal in quality in anything that has been done up to this time by any one writing to-day.

The story-teller's story is not a story of events or experiences it is a story of existence, and the fact that the story teller exists makes a story and keeps on making a story. The story-teller's story will live because the story-teller is alive. As he is alive and as his gift is the complete expression of that life it will continue to live.

1925

TROUBADOUR

[Review of *Troubadour* by Alfred Kreymborg.]

There are many histories of us then and now and they are written now and they are often written now. Many histories of us are often written now. Sometimes in the histories of us each one of us is different from the others of us and the one writing the history of himself and us is different in his history of himself and us from us. In this history of us of himself and us Kreymborg makes us makes himself and each one of us different enough so that some one can know us. That is very nice for him and for us and very pleasant for him and for us and very satisfying to him and to us. We are all pleased with him and with us and so we say that he has made a very good description of himself and of each one of us. A history of himself and of each one of us and connections of more than one of us is a very sensitive thing a sensitive history of himself and of each one of us and of some who are ones and one. Always this is a good thing.

1925

OSCAR WILDE DISCOVERS AMERICA

[Review of *Oscar Wilde Discovers America*
by Lloyd Lewis and Henry Austin Smith.]

To Lloyd Lewis who when all is said,
makes them alive and makes them dead.

It is a completely fascinating book and I have read every word
of it. It is a fascinating book because Lewis finds fascinating every
detail that is American. When I was in Chicago to see "Pinafore,"
Lewis leaned over to me excitedly, do you see the little midship-
man, yes, he's cute I said. Farragut was that and wore exactly that
uniform said Lewis sinking back. That is the way he is about any
detail that is American and that is why his books are fascinating.

In this one I have had a special pleasure, I went as a little girl
from Baltimore to California just about the year he is describing
and my memory makes it feel just like that and it was just like
that. Then having just gone lecturing all over America it makes
everything that happened to Oscar Wilde be real because fifty
years after it was still just like that. When I was in America they
asked me if I did not find America changed and I said no of course
not what could they change to when they are just like that.

It was airplanes instead of trains and good roads instead of bad
ones, but the newspaper might almost have been exactly the same
ones and the reporters exactly the same ones and all the people
after all being so interested and so kind and so nice and the country just the same and the pleasure of everybody just the same. No
America has not changed. The newspapers have to be funny just
the same way and in the same way the funny poems are funny but
the funny prose is not very funny. After all to be funny is very
difficult, there is really less good funny writing written than any
other writing so why should anybody who writes for any newspaper
think he can be funny. And Oscar Wilde wondered that too.

It is a wonderful book, as I said they make them alive and they
make them dead, and that is the American thing, nobody but an
American writer ever makes anybody really dead, and Lloyd Lewis
does he makes them dead. There are a lot of people that are really
dead in the book, and they are as alive as they are dead, which is
a very interesting thing.

Only once did the authors break down and get into the game,

that is on page three hundred and fifty when they say, how this philosophy would have delayed the settlement of the west was a question he did not face. Why should he face something that did not concern him, it was a pleasure to the west that they got settled up so fast but not any pleasure to him. That is the only time in the whole book that the authors stop the picture to get into the argument, and that is what makes the book so extraordinary the picture remains a picture. Wilde and America and the picture is never other than a complete picture except for this one solitary sentence. And it is not like any other thing that has been written because the picture they make is a complete picture every second of it being a picture. There is no remembering it is something they see and they are always seeing it, and so I think it is the most interesting historical book that has yet been written in America, and indeed they control the time so well that even with the thing Wilde was to say when he got home the picture keeps being there as a single thing.

Of course it interests me a lot because the time sense in writing history is awfully hard to manage because most historians remember their material but Lewis does not, it is there present to him all the time and at any time any detail is as present as any whole and there it is as it is.

The photographs are most interesting, the one of Lillian Russell is wonderful and the one, and that is not polite because I did not loan it I gave it to Lloyd Lewis, the one of Mrs. Jesse James, it is all so real and all of it is not illustration but part of what it is. Lloyd Lewis never has to remember because anything that is American is in him and he is in it.

1926

SIR FRANCIS ROSE

Each generation composes its pictures, that is to say composes not by what they do but what they see, by what they feel. And yet it is after all one and just at the same time there are those who are here if you like as one.

But not at all.

There is one, after seeing that there is a generation and having the evidence that there is a composition one often is mistaken not about that but about which one it is because dates are undated now as well as then. This introduces Francis Rose this a painter probably a younger one. Of this I am certain.

help for a young painter

1932

SIR FRANCIS ROSE

I have told a number of things about Francis Rose and now I will tell about how he painted at Bilignin. I said to him then Hokusai used to speak of himself as an old man who loved to paint. Francis Rose could speak of himself as a young man who loves to paint. He loves to paint. He does love to paint. He is happy when he paints, he paints with both hands, he paints, he just paints. He painted eleven pictures in eight days and do not think they were not painted, they were, each one was, each one was all painted. And so he painted Bilignin which is here and the waterfall of Lucy Church Amiably which is here and he has been painting ever since then because that was a year and a half ago and his painting does not stop. He likes to paint and more than that the painting he paints needs and likes to be painted. It all amounts to that.

Since then yes he has been painting and as he is a young man coming to be a grown man he is beginning not only to paint but to come to paint what he is going to paint, and what is that. In a little picture which he has just sent me which is a going on of what he has known of himself he has commenced to know that the inside is outside and that the outside is inside and that that is true of what he is to paint.

1934

a young painter

STEIGLITZ

If anything is done and something is done then somebody has to do it.

Or somebody has to have done it.

That is Stieglitz's way.

He has done it.

He remembers very well our first meeting.

But not better than I do.

Oh no not better than I do.

He was the first one that ever printed anything that I had done.

And you can imagine what that meant to me or to any one.

I remember him dark and I felt him having white hair.

He can do both of these things or anything.

Now that sounds as if it were the same thing or not a difficult thing but it is it just is, it is a difficult thing to do two things as one, but he just can that is what Stieglitz is and he is important to every one oh yes he is whether they know it or not oh yes he is.

There are some who are important to every one whether any one knows anything of that one or not and Stieglitz is such a one, he is that one, he is indeed, there is no question but that he is such a one no question indeed, but that he is one, who is an important one for every one, no matter whether they do or whether they do not know anything about any such thing about any such one about him.

That is what Stieglitz is.

Any one can recognize him.

Any one does know that there are such ones, all of us do know that Stieglitz is such a one.

That he is one.

291.

I am sorry that I can not go on longer and tell all about and more and more what Stieglitz is, but they never told me what they were all doing because Stieglitz had said do not bother her she is in France, but now just in time and I am so glad I find out I could just say what I know, I like to say what I know, and how could I know, how could I not know what Stieglitz is.

a famous photographer   1934

PICABIA

When Picabia came to see us in the country we talked about a great many things: we told each other a great many things! Among other things he told me that his grandfather who brought him up and with whom he lived, was one of the inventors of photography. He was a friend and companion of Daguerre, who invented the daguerreotype. Picabia, when he was a young boy was always with his grandfather. They used to travel a great deal and always visited museums and his grandfather, who was doing experiments in coloured photography at that time, being a well-known savant, was always given permission to photograph. So they photographed all day and they developed all night, and this his early experience, so Picabia believes, and I am not sure he is not right, has had a good deal to do with the development of modern painting. Picabia got from the constant contact with photography, which gradually bored him very much in spite of his admiration and affection for his grandfather, got something which did give him the idea of transparence and four dimensional painting, and this through him certainly has a great deal to do with everything. Even now in his later painting and certainly in his drawing he has achieved a transparence which is peculiarly a thing that has nothing to do with the surface seen.

1934

ELIE LASCAUX

Elie Lascaux lived with his mother in a village and he had heard of stoves but never seen one, he always all his life hoped to have one. All his young life he had lived with an open fireplace for cooking and heating and anybody who has lived with one knows how cold any very young one or any one can be with one. Now he has an apartment that is steam-heated so he has never had a stove but he still dreams of one. When he came to Paris he was a very young man seventeen years old then and he was all alone and he went to the Arc de Triomphe to see everything and he naturally got there. He watched the automobiles going round round and around the arch and each time he thought it was the same one, that it was a merry go round and a most splendid one. Slowly he saw that each time it was a different one and slowly then he knew what Paris was it was a place where there were so many automobiles that each one that passed him was a different one.

All this made a Paris for him and he gets it into his pictures the white light of his pictures all the Paris that he discovered then.

It is quite an extraordinary thing that every year in painting his painting is more beautiful and developing and yet never is there left out of it the thing he saw then, when he was a young one.

His painting has a white light that is a light and anything a village, green trees any part of Paris, Bourges, all and any french thing can be in that white light which is the light that Elie Lascaux has inside him.

1935

SIR FRANCIS ROSE

Sir Francis Rose was born in 1909 on the 18th of September at Moore Park, Surrey, just before noon in the middle of a thunderstorm.

He was brought up by his Scotch grandmother. His father died when he was five. Later on he was sent to various schools but he always ran away and came back to his grandmother.

From the beginning he always painted, and he always went to museums he just could not help it, and at thirteen he began to travel with a tutor, he had already begun to write a long history of the early Italian primitives and he went on and on drawing and painting and looking at things in museums.

His grandmother died when he was nineteen and he went on travelling and painting, painting and travelling.

The first time a picture of his was publicly shown was in London when he was thirteen at a show organised by Sargent and Orpen for painters under the age of fifteen, he had a gold medal for his painting.

His first important exhibition was in Paris when he was twenty-two when he showed one hundred pictures. This year at the age of twenty-nine his pictures were shown, fifty of them, at the Musée du Petit Palais and one was bought by the Musée.

I believe that Francis Rose is the most important painter among the young painters painting to-day. Every country has its turn. In the nineteenth century it was French painters who created painting, in the beginning of the twentieth century it was Spanish painers who created painting and now towards the middle of the twentieth century it is an Englishman who is creating the important painting of his time.

Francis Rose is a painter who is recreating life in colors, in many colors. English people have always loved colors, and at last in Francis Rose they have a painter who makes the colors English people love by painting. It is the first time it has happened and it is very important, his compositions live in colors, his drawing lives in colors, and it is all completely alive.

1939

SHERWOOD'S SWEETNESS

Yes undoubtedly, Sherwood Anderson had a sweetness, and sweetness is rare. Once or twice somebody is sweet, but everything in Sherwood was made of this sweetness. Here in war-time France they have made a new sugar, grape sugar, and it is as sweet as sugar and it has all through it the tang of a grape. That was Sherwood's sweetness, it was like that.

I had a letter from him, just before he died, and when I read the letter, well it just said how do you do and how are you and glad to have heard from you, but all of it had this quality of sugar made out of grapes, it just naturally was this grape sugar substance in everything Sherwood did or was. And he was everything and he did everything.

Funny I always connect Sherwood with sweet fruits. I remember in New Orleans when he came into the room he had a bag of oranges, twenty-five for twenty-five cents, and he and we ate all the twenty-five oranges; they were orange sweet, the kind that are twenty-five oranges for twenty-five cents [?always] are orange sweet.

Dear Sherwood, as long as grape sugar is grape sugar and it always is, and oranges twenty-five for twenty-five cents are oranges, so long will Sherwood be Sherwood. And as grape sugar will always be, and oranges will always be, so will he.

One cannot cry when grape sugar is like that or twenty-five oranges for twenty-five cents are like that, and one cannot die when they are like that, so one does not cry for Sherwood nor does Sherwood die.

No.

Grape sugar and oranges twenty-five for twenty-five cents, they are Sherwood.

1941

FROM DARK TO DAY

There were dark days when we first knew Pierre Balmain. We met his mother in '39 at Aix-les-Bains, and she said she had a son up there in the army in the snows of Savoy, and he read my books; would I dedicate him one. Naturally I was pleased, and then came '40 and the deafeat, and we wondered about Pierre Balmain whom we had never seen but who was up there in the snows, and then at last we heard he was safe, and then he was back, and then we met him. He used to come over on his bicycle; we were many miles away, but nobody minded that, and the winter was cold and we were cold, and he made us some nice warm suits and a nice warm coat, and Alice Toklas insists that one of her suits was as wonderful as any he was showing at his opening, and there was no reason why not, after all, didn't he design it, and didn't he come over on his bicycle to oversee, and was it not as it all just is in dark days? There are bright spots. Well, we got to know him better and better, some children played some of my plays, and he showed us the chic of making a very tall girl taller by putting her on a footstool. These were nice days in those dark days, and then Pierre used to go to and fro from Paris, and he brought us back a breath of our dear Paris and also darning cotton to darn our stockings and our linen, that was Pierre, and then he kept moving around as young men had to do in those days, not to be sent away into Germany, and then there was the liberation, and then in Paris here we all were, and Pierre just full of what he was going to do, and we were sure he would do it, and he has. I suppose there at the opening we were the only ones who had been clothed in all those long years in Pierre Balmain's clothes, we were proud of it. It is nice to know the young man when he is just a young man and nobody knows, and now, well, I guess very soon now anybody will know. And we were so pleased and proud. Yes, we were.

1945

RAOUL DUFY

One must meditate about pleasure. Raoul Dufy is pleasure. To know to know to love her so. You have to really love what is to have pleasure and Dufy does really love what is and we have the pleasure.

I came back to Paris after the long sad years of the occupation. I will tell all about that, and I wandered around the streets the way I do and there in a window were a lot of etchings and there so pleasantly was one by Dufy, it was an etching of kitchen utensils, in an inspired circle and at the bottom was a lovely roasted chicken, God bless him, wouldn't he just have a lovely etching by him in the window of a shop and of lots of kitchen utensils, the factories could not make them but he had, and the roast chicken, how often during those dark days was I homesick for the quays of Paris and a roast chicken.

Dufy and wars. I remember it was just at the end of the last war 1919, and we were at the first salon d'automne and there unexpectedly was a sofa and fauteuils and chairs, and the material was a design by Dufy, it was shock of pleasure, there it was a pleasure. Wars are sad but Dufy is in their midst a shock of pleasure. I often wonder who has that sofa, I would like to see it again, it was so real a pleasure, after a war, so real a pleasure.

Wars and Dufy. Once again.

We were in Culoz, not far from Aix-les-Bains and as enemy foreigners of course we were not supposed to take trains but we could always get permission to go and see a dentist or a doctor and so we went to Aix-les-Bains very often. Carl van Vechten used to call them in the high day of their liveliness the sad streets of Aix-les-Bains, and they were kind of sad, those going up into the hills and down into the lake and not much lived in and the sizes a little square for their length, yes we did see what Carl meant when he called them the sad streets of Aix-les-Bains, but we liked them, we were used to them and we liked them and everybody was friendly and we had liked them for a good many years and now it was war that is to say not war but occupation, Aix-les-Bains was occupied by the Germans but we like the French had learned not to know they were there and the streets of Aix-les-Bains were as they always had been, yes they were, after all they were and then one day we were on the terrace having a drink of something, even in those dark days, one could get a drink of something on the terrace, something that was not Aix-les- Bains water and there also sitting on the terrace in the sunshine was Dufy, his hair white white and his face rosy and his color like his color is when he paints other things, naturally a painter paints the way he is made up in color, I do think that is so, indeed I do know that it is so, the colors that made up the painter when you look at him are the colors he naturally uses when he paints anything. And there was Dufy as delightful in color as the color he paints and we were so delighted to see one another, there were a great many there some French and many Germans but we were alone together quite alone and quite together. He had been to Paris we had not, and there was so much to tell and he told it a little a little and a little and every little was what he told and then he said he would take the train and we would lunch together he coming to us, and he did and there we sat on our terrace in Culoz in the sunshine and ate our lunch together, and it was all his color as naturally it would be and we spent a pleasant time together, and we were ourselves, which was a pleasure. And then he went away, anyway to meet again any day.

Then we in Culoz, Ain, along with most of France, were liberated in August and September of 1944. It was wonderful to be liberated.

For several months, we were so busy just being excited and being liberated that we did not think of Paris. Yes, in the darkest days of the occupation I was very homesick for Paris, I used to say that I was homesick for the quays of Paris and for a roast chicken, a roast chicken and the quays of Paris. Now every day I walk up and down the quays of Paris and the other day a friend took us to a restaurant and there we ate, perhaps we should not have, but we did eat, we ate a whole roast chicken. Basket, the white poodle, got the bones. So for us the liberation was complete and we are in Paris.

As I say, for two months in Culoz, and almost three, we were so busy just feeling free and talking to everybody who was feeling free too, that we almost forgot about going back to Paris, and then we began to think about coming back, and we began to write to everybody to ask whether we could exist if we did come back. Some said we could and some said we could not. Some said that there was no light, no food and no gas and that it was all dark and dreary, and some said it was very pleasant but no food, but plenty of gas and light, and others said it was very pleasant and plenty of everything and finally they wrote to us that the Gestapo in the month of August of '44 had been in the apartment, and what was the state of the apartment nobody seemed to want to say, and we were nervous. It was easy to be nervous.

All through the war I had been superstitious, I had not wanted anyone to mention the apartment, to mention anything in it, it would be kind of safer that way, and then finally someone wrote that it was all right but frightfully dirty and then finally someone found the nice Russian exile who had always cleaned our house when we came back and closed it up when we left, and he apparently had weathered the storm and he had started to work, and in three weeks our apartment would be as lovely as ever, and so we made up our mind to come, and to come back the middle of December. It was cold, and there were floods, and we had to have a camion and a taxi, a wood-burning one, and we had to pack, and we did not know whether to bring up everything we had accumulated in those five years or to give them away and finally we decided to bring up almost everything, and we did, luckily we did.

We in the taxi were to start earlier, that is to say at midnight, and the camion later, that is to say a daybreak, and we started.

It was midnight, and we left the country, and for us the war was over, we were taking the road to Paris, would we remember it, what it was like.

There was no more war there in the middle of December, but there were floods, and the first thing we could not do was to take the regular road to Bourg, so the driver decided to go by Hauteville and climb through the pass and then go merrily on to Bourg. It was midnight, and we climbed and climbed, and then there was snow on the ground and the driver jumped out and the car went on and he pushed it on with a sort of dancing run. It was strange, and we felt strange, and then the car stopped, pushing was no more use, so he said he could back down the hill, that scared me so I got out and walked, but the others, not being used to driving, were not scared, to be backed down that hill in the snow in the midnight dark. It was strange, peace was being stranger than war. Since I have been back in Paris I have asked a lot of American drivers if they could back down a twisting road at night in the snow for three kilometers, and they said they would not like to. At least we were back to where we started from and decided to go by Lyon, that road was foggy and strange too, everything was strange, not being either awake or asleep, it was strange. I cheered myself up with American K rations. They are sustaining, crackers, sugar, candy and a touch of lemon, very comforting.

Every now and then the tires, they were ersatz tires, and that backing in the snow was not good for them, and so every hour or two they burst, and the driver only had an ersatz jack, so it got longer and longer being on the road, and it was night again before we got to Fontainebleau.

It was very mysterious going over all those roads, over which I had driven so often, they looked quite natural, they were surprisingly all there, all the pieces of road that I remembered so well, only now I was being driven in a charcoal-burning taxi and being sustained by K rations. That was all the difference.

It was getting later and later and nearer and nearer, and we were all pretty well asleep when someone stopped the car. They were three FFI men and one woman and the woman had a gun on her back, not the men. That was quite different to what we were accustomed. They asked the driver for his papers and they were satisfied, and then they asked me. I said I was American. Well, said they, there are Germans. Not me, said I indignantly, giving him my papers. All right, he said, and looking into the back where were Alice Toklas and the little servant we were bringing up from the country. Miss Toklas said with dignity she was an American, and she, he said, pointing to the maid, she out of her sleep woke up and said, sir, I am a Savoyard. Oh yes, he said, and all these bundles, said he. Oh those, I said, are meat and butter and eggs. Now don't touch them, they are all carefully packed, and enough to keep us a week in Paris. Ah, yes, he said, and this big thing. That, said Miss Toklas, with decision, is a Picasso painting, don't touch it. I congratulate you, said the FFI, and waved us on.

So then soon it was the gates of Paris and was it real. Yes, there it was, the same as always, and I got quite excited, and told the driver where to go and sent him wrong, naturally, but we backed in and we backed out and finally I saw the Lion of Belfort and the Boulevard Raspail, and we could not go wrong then, it must be Paris, and it was dark, but we did find our way and there at last was the Rue Christine, and out we got and in we came. Yes, it was the same, so much more beautiful, but it was the same.

All the pictures were there, the apartment was all there, and it was all clean and beautiful. We just looked, and then everybody running in, the concierge, the husband of the laundress downstairs, the secretary of our landlord, the bookbinder, they all came rushing in to say how do you do and to tell us about the visit of the Gestapo, their stamp was still on the door.

I did not want to know, because knowing is frightening, but I had to know, and it is interesting. One way and another the apartment had not been troubled, it being a part of town and with an entrance that does not look like a good apartment and also it was not on the Rue de Fleurus mentioned in the Autobiography of Alice Toklas, but somehow some Gestapo in August 1944 heard of it. They broke in. The secretary of the proprietor, who has a book-binding establishment below us, heard them walking about in the apartment. She suspected that it was the Gestapo, but she did not come up to see, she telephoned to the French police and said robbers had broken into the house. The French police came twenty strong and everybody asked for their papers and they were not in order. They had no authority to enter this apartment, so the police, feeling strong in August 1944, told them to get out and they went, after flourishing a photograph of me in the air and saying they would find me. They also went off with the keys, which was not noticed, and the next day at noon they came in while everybody was away and they stole linen and dresses and shoes and kitchen utensils and dishes and bed covers and pillows, but no pictures and no furniture, and they broke nothing, strange to say, whereupon the secretary had the locksmith change the locks, and that was that.

It was all over, it was very frightening, the apartment was very lovely, the treasures were all there, and we went to sleep, quite a little frightened, but still asleep, not warm nor cold, a little tepid and on the whole very happy.

And the next day was the next day, and I began to say, how many days are there in a week. So nice.

I walked and I walked, and Basket, my dog, and I are still walking, my dog and I. The first thing that struck me in Paris after the miracle that it was Paris and was all there was that there were so many dogs in Paris, and lots of them such big dogs, too, and not so very young. I began to ask everybody about it. I talk to everybody in Paris just as I do in the country, that is one of the nice things about Paris. Well, we talked dogs and they explained, well one way and another way you did keep your dog, sometimes the restaurants gave you leftovers, or the butcher, or your dog was a great favorite in the street and you put out a basket and people put in scraps, one way and another you did go on keeping your dog. I walked and I walked, and I am still walking. Paris is so lovely. Twice now I have come back to it, saved and beautifully lovely. In the last war, after being in London at the outbreak, we came back to Paris 1914, came back on a moonlight night, and there it was, all lovely and saved, and this time, even though the

Germans had been there, it was all lovely and saved.

Picasso had been impatiently awaiting our return. He came in the next morning and we were very moved when we embraced, and we kept saying it is a miracle, all the treasures which made our youth, the pictures, the drawings, the objects, all there.

I began to think that the whole thing was a nightmare, it wasn't true, we had just been away for a summer vacation and had come back. Every little shop was there with its same proprietor, the shops that had been dirty were still dirty, the shops that had been clean before the war were still clean, all the little antiquity shops were there, each with the same kinds of things in it that there used to be, because each little antiquity shop runs to its own kind of antiquities. It was a miracle, it was a miracle.

And then I walked and I walked, and the architecture began to impress me so much more than it ever had, it was no longer a background, but a reality. I realized that architecture was made for people who go about on their feet, that that is what architecture is made for. How lovely it all was, and the quays of the Seine.

Then there were such funny things, the German are funny. They took down some statues and not others, they left, strangely enough, a bronze Lafayette given by the school children of America, and they left an enormous large statue of King Albert with all its inscription about the last war, and strangest of all, they did not touch the inscription upon the arch in the Tuilleries with the horses on top of it and on which is carved, When the voice of the conqueror of Austerlitz was heard the German empire was dead. They certainly are funny people, the Germans.

And then there are the soldiers, who wander eternally, wander about the streets, they do funny things. The other day I was watching one look at the reflection of the Louvre in a glass shop window. He said he seemed to get it better that way. I talk to them all, they seem to like it, and I certainly do. At first I hesitated a bit, it's all right, everybody seems to have plenty of time, of course, when you have to walk so much you must have plenty of time. And so we are back in Paris, yes back in Paris. How often has Paris been saved, how often. Yes, I walk around Paris, we all walk around Paris all day long and night too. Everybody is walking around Paris, it is very nice. How many days are there in a week so nice. Very many, happily, very many.

To know to know to love her so, yes Paris.

Do not think that Paris is lovely because it is, not at all.

How well I remember during the last war, one day it was a sad rainy day and we were walking past one of the Army hospitals near the Montparnasse, and Picasso said, there were American soldiers standing around the entrance this was 1917-18 and Picasso said they don't like Paris, they say is this Paris, but what they do not understand said Picasso is that this is Paris, all right they don't like Paris, they are right, they don't like Paris.

After all well you got to be faithful to what you love when it is bedraggled and sad and weepy and dirty as well as when it is chic. What is a city, well of course it is made up of people in it, after all, no French people no Paris, no father and mother no child, all the same, the child has something that does not come out of the father and mother or even grandfathers and grandmothers, it is different, whatever resemblances there are, it is different, well a city is like that, it is made by all the people in it but it is itself in what it is over and beyond what it is made by the people who made it, yes it is.

To know to know to love her so, yes Paris.

We were made by Paris all of us and even when we do not meet we are each part of what Paris has made us. Everybody who has been really made by Paris is one with us because each one of us was made by that Paris that did make each and every one of us. That is why there is no need of our seeing each other and that is what always surprises the people who live in other cities and other capitals, that everybody who belongs should naturally always be there when any other one is there, but not at all, each one of us lives apart and perhaps for years we do not see or hear of one another, if so pleasant, if not also pleasant, why worry, when pleasantness is so pleasant. Remember one must meditate about pleasure. We are all pleasure all of us made by Paris we are all pleasure, and I tell you again and again how naturally Raoul Dufy is a pleasure.

It is so natural for any of us to see each other it is so natural for any of us not to see each other.

Well Marie Laurencin and I we had not met for so many years and we met and she said she would like to paint Basket the poodle and we met and we liked her painting Basket, she likes to paint white or brown dogs and dogs with long hair, she does not paint short-haired dogs or black dogs, I assure you I really do assure you that any painter paints the color that they are really and truly. Remember that.

And so Basket was posing very well, from time to time to be sure I had to support his chin, dogs have a tendency to find their heads get heavy and to have to have their chin supported. Well while the painting was going on young people came in. Young people like old people, they do, they do not like middle-aged people, not generally but they do like old people and that is all right it is mutual, old people like them. There is a natural affiliation between age and youth, which there is not with middle age and youth or middle age and age. All right, young people like us and they come to see us and they like to listen to us. And so while Basket was having his portrait painted the young men and women came and sat around and they asked about Guillaume Apollinaire and that was natural enough, and Marie talked and I talked and gradually as we talked we realized that it was not the people that we had known that had formed us but the streets of Paris, the Paris that is made of streets and rivers and islands and hills and people pushing things along or pulling things along and wagons and markets and fruits and vegetables and mist and trees and buildings, and long streets in the dark, and short streets and squares in the light, and everything that makes Paris what it is.

No it was not people we had known, actually in those days we did not know anybody, nobody knew anybody, we came from foreign countries and knew nobody, others came from the provinces of France and knew nobody, and just a very few knew each other by accident, somehow, and we did not go to the theatre or to visit, yes the circus, of course in those days the circus, and a bistro a very little café where there was nobody except the people always there and never anybody else, and the buses, and the long dimness, there was a great deal of dimness of fog, of mist in those days, now that one is older there is more sunshine and more clear sky, anything can be true, but yes it was Paris. Paris that had an existence in and by itself not made of people, to be sure people are always there but really not made of people. Museums a little bit but not too much. I just saw the other day a picture that Dufy had painted which was a copy of Renoir's Moulin de la Galette. That is the way it is Renoir had painted it and the Paris that was Renoir's was not the Paris that was ours, but it was the Paris that belonged to Paris. There again Renoir had made it large Dufy had made it small, Renoir had made them round Dufy had made them delicate, Renoir had made them red, Dufy had made them green and rose, and yet it was the same picture it really was. Marie Laurencin and I talked about those days and how Paris had made us, we did not make Paris, although we were adding adding what we had to add, but all the time Paris was doing its own adding, adding what it had to add, and so with all that adding something is added and being added adds.

Then came the occupation. That we did not see, the last time that we saw Paris was in the fall of 1939, and then we never saw it again until everything was over.

So many American soldiers came to Paris and did not know that it was Paris, they did not know what had been added and they thought everything was gone, but no nothing was gone only so much had been added.

They did not know, but as it was it was Paris. I too wanted to know what had been added. I did not know at first that it was at all changed, it was just as naturally it as it ever had been and then slowly I knew. First there were the plaques, sometimes yellow marble just a little plaque sometimes white, and on each one here fell fighting such and such and his age, and they were not mostly not such young men, 25 to 40, and of course the really young they were too far away to have fought in the streets of Paris, they were either in Germany or in the hills, but slowly and then quite suddenly they blossomed out like flowers on the street corners the plaques that told of how here one had died and then there one had died, one by one they had died in that Paris and for that Paris, where a great many one by one had died, and gradually it was still the natural Paris I had always known but there had been four years of its life that I had not known. My friends told me but I had not known, I had known France yes I had not missed anything of France during that time but I had missed something of Paris that others had known. Picasso was a little sorry for me and so was Marie, and I understood that they were a little sorry for me. Dufy had told me a little but he too had been away and those who had not been shut in inside the walls of Paris for those six years well yes we do miss something, something was added while we were away, something. They all try to tell me about that something and I have come back to another something, and yet during my lifetime Paris did add something while I was not there while it was adding that something and Paris knows it, not about me but it knows it. Sometime everybody will know it, it does happen that way. Paris can wait until everybody knows it.

I think well naturally I think about painting about everybody's painting what they paint, that too does something to Paris the way they are all any day and everyday the way they are all painting it in every way. Those who can paint side by side with those who can't paint, no painter is so great a painter that he cannot sit on

71

his little camp stool and settle himself down beside the Seine and paint, the Seine that so many of the Americans said was a dirty river, is it, well bless the Seine River. As I say I think a great deal about painting and what is the painting that a painter paints. But first I think well naturally I first think about how a writer writes, that is natural enough. A writer does not write with his ears or his mouth, he writes with his eyes. It is his eyes that make his writing, sound is not of any interest to him, ears and mouth useless from the standpoint of writing, all he needs are his eyes and his hand, that is all, he can hear and talk all he wants but he writes with his eyes and his hand. That is the reason radios are so rotten from the standpoint of a writer. Now that's for a writer and when I said that to Picasso he said of course the mouths of all writers you can see it in the portraits are always tight shut and he pointed to mine. Well anyway it is true, and now about painters, with what do they paint. Well one of the things they do not paint is what their eyes see. Painters talk about abstract painting but as I was saying and funnily enough it was seeing Dufy at Aix-les-Bains made me realize it, painters do not paint the colors that their eyes see, they paint the colors of which they themselves are composed. There is a great deal of nonsense talked about painting, musicians and architects and writers do not talk about abstraction, they know perfectly well that everything they do is an abstraction, but painters because they have to use their eyes to work with labor under the delusion that they use their eyes to see the things they paint and so they think that they must get away from painting what they think they see by being abstract, but oh dear me, what they paint when they think they are most straightforwardly painting what they see has nothing whatsoever to do with what they see, think of Dufy, nobody calls him abstract but he is he does not paint what he sees, he paints what he is, and certainly it is not what anybody else sees. It is all so false, this idea that painters paint what they see, they use their eyes in order to paint what they know just as writers use their eyes to write what they know, but what you see, of course you don't see it, think of Dufy think of any painter of course he is abstract, he abstracts the colors of which he is made and he puts them down in the light and shade of which he is made and his eyes have very little to do with it, except to work with. It is all so foolish. That is it is foolish not to know all this which is undoubtedly so.

And so this is what life is and it is a pleasure, the constant abstracting the color of which a painter is made is a constant pleasure it is a pleasure to him and it is a pleasure to any other.

And now a last word. We were all young and we more or less knew one another and each one of us had something to say that added something to the other. And we meet and we feel and we do what each one of us has to do, and one thing we all have to do we have to do what we have to do and in doing what we have to do we are in a continuous state of pleasure.

One must meditate about pleasure. Dufy is pleasure. Think of the color and it is not that and the line and it is not that, but it is that which is all together and which is the color that is in Dufy, when he sits in the sunshine, there it is in him, to be sure he has to have abstracted it out of him before you can see it in him, but I don't know perhaps one did even see it in him before he had completely abstracted it out of him.

We have to meditate about pleasure.

That is one of the things that we who abstract things have, we are never bored we are always in a state of pleasure. And I always think of Dufy and the etching of the kitchen utensils and the sofa and the Moulin de la Galette, war, rheumatism no nothing touches it, it is always in a state of pleasure.

One must meditate about pleasure. Raoul Dufy is pleasure.

1946

73

III

Nature and the Emotions

Whereas human beings and human actions were the content of the portraits, nature and human nature are the content of Gertrude Stein's "Romantic Period." The new ingredients are the emotions as they play about the pleasant domestic scenes of country life.

In "Vacations in Brittany" there are birds, rabbits, hens, dogs and cows; there are houses, walls, crockery and furniture; there are figs and ferns, lettuce and hay; there are the sea, the stones, the woods, the potato fields; there are families, servants, men, boys and saints. That is Brittany.

In "Ireland" a children's rhyme sets up a kind of slapping game which is like the back and forth of a dance or country ritual. The introduction of implied movement prefigures the "landscape play" developed by Gertrude Stein at this time. Rituals are continued in "Dinner," "Readings" and "Today We Have a Vacation" in a domestic setting. "Mildred's Thoughts" take place in a landscape of romantic beauty. So does "Procession." A movement of thoughts; a movement of orderly crowds.

"If He Thinks": "How many stories are there in it?" This is the leit-motif *for the later* Four Saints in Three Acts: *"How many acts are there in it"? There is also an interlude of love poetry: "I don't think I know why I love my baby so . . ." Rhymed passages alternate with paragraphs of prose. Either way the story behind the story is fraught with emotion: seizing, freezing, following, shrinking, overflowing, grieving, deserting, shaming, protesting, pleasing—what more of a story can one want?*

VACATION IN BRITTANY

KING OR KANGAROO KING OR YELLOW KING OR MARIE CLAIRE SUGGESTS A MEADOW. AND THE USE OF THOUGHT

BY THE SEA

By the sea inland smell the goose, by the figs George buy the figs. By the crown, Sylvester has the crown and glory constant glory. And in the midst of the speed in the rising of the stones stones do not rise of themselves unless they are made to resemble the wood in the midst of stones and salt can we can we declare when a house was built. A house is built either in the shape of a lamb of a heart or of a bush. And almost immediately the walls scale. They whiten and the sun changes chinese red to blue.

Immerse yourself.

LEAVES ME LEAVES ME

Why can you muster men and birds. Why can you whistle so shyly. And why do you mention harm. No eyes can make thirds and no rabbits can cheer. It does them good to be sold. Who sells hens. Connect the impression that earliness and repetition and even octagons are necessary to families. Families really need a fern. Ferns are really seen by their leaves. Whole dogs have trimming. They trim their size. One cannot be merry in peace. And in war. Who can care to wear what is there and in there. Who can carry a nest to the hay. Who can say yes how do you do yesterday. Can you have lettuce, can you have the best figs in a servant.

To serve in a sieve and a saint. To paint and to see all the sea. To see electricity.

CONSCIENCE

Racket is a noise. Noise is a poise. Boys with the b spelled like a p is poise. Boys is poise.

And then I read the men. Men say. Leave me and be gay. Men

say tenderness to-day. Men say go away.

And leave me.

A potato field and the promised land. It is a very pleasant burning smell.

Armandine Armandine yesterday noon. Armandine Armandine what is the tune.

Devotion. What is devotion. He is devoted to that. She is devout. And an opening. An opening is covered by Cæsars. Sharp wire. Do sharpen wire. Devotion. Devotion is determined by design.

When this you see remember me.

I do mean to replace crockery with furniture. I do mean to organise victory. I do mean to say grace.

I am not a bar tender.

Automatically but not silently.

Little fool little stool little fool for me. Little stool little fool little stool for me. And what is a stool. That was the elegant name for a cow. Little stool little fool little stool for me. Little fool little stool for me.

Let us let us conscience.

Let us let us conscientiously renounce the sense of reticence.

1920

IRELAND

Peas porridge hot
Peas porridge cold
Peas porridge in the pot
Nine days old.
Have soldiers there
Have niggers here
Have suppers everywhere
We forbid fear.
Have butter hot
Have sugar cold
Have water in the pot
To love the bold.
Have noises squeak
Have voices thin
Have girls have a horse
Have a day win.
Have a viscount for me
Have a release
Have a suggestion then
Of a bêtise.
Have a real odor
And the respect
Have a collection then
Of the way that,
Of the way that you know
How to rule me
Have a way to say now
We are what then.
You are it is a muss
You are polite.
I dont say this of you
No not to-night.
And it is true indeed
That we can sing.
We of our country dear
Liberating.

1920

DINNER

Pigeons.
Who kills pigeons.
Turkeys.
Who eats turkeys.
Chickens.
Who earns chickens.
Oysters.
Who smells oysters.
Lobsters.
Who destroys lobsters.
Christmas.
Who imitates wood.
Central dogs.
Who are women.
Love of race.
Who mends tables.
Turn away.
Who has shells.
What do shells make.
   Shells make a charming scene and a baby a little baby with a lamb.
   It is a nice day and moon.

1921

READINGS

Kisses can kiss us
A duck a hen and fishes, followed by wishes.
Happy little pair.

1921

TODAY WE HAVE A VACATION

Cæsars. What are Cæsars. Cæsars are round a little longer than wide but not oval. They are picturesque and useful.

Birds. What are birds. Birds are in the trees and realize that. They do not protect a hat. They have needles.

And what is coaxing.
Coaxing is George and Marion and Alice and Julian and Harry and Paul.

Believe in dolphins.

A great many people believe in dophins who do not believe in dolmans or dolomites or marble or composition or queens or even the eighteenth century.

And the seventeenth century.

Eighteen thirty two is not the seventeenth century.

And then breathe spaniels.

Nowadays pekinese are led about by maids or elderly women. A great many love chinamen. Do you mean love them. They describe them. I describe them differently. I say they dress well. And what is their resemblance. Their resemblance is to us.

1921

MILDRED'S THOUGHTS

Pigeons cooing only open cards and cases.

And when does grain yellow and the vegetables.

How horribly we crowned the evergreens. We always used to say that we lived in an aquarium. And now how silently the sun shines with a warm wind and cherished water. How livelily we chalk the earth and it opens. How can opening be feeble.

Caroline do not be religious do not be religiously free. Do not love hopes and pearls. I know you don't.

I think, I think I think that it is a victory a victory of force over intelligence and I I I do not agree, I think it is a victory a victory.

Can you hope for the rest.

And now let us tell how it affects me.

Can you tumble out.

I suppose I pose I expose, I repose, I close the door when the sun shines so, I close the door when the wind is so strong and the dust is not there but there is a glare, how tenderly I sun. The fuchsia how can you enclose a fuchsia, the fuchsia has learned this that Caroline loves her sister and will neglect the fuchsia for her sister. I mention this not to displease Henrietta because in all things I obey Henrietta.

How did she weaken Ireland. Give a thought to them, and give them my thoughts. Tell them to remember that every eleven years the sun shines hotly and also bid them remember that a farmer's life is a hard hard life a farmer's life for me.

Establish curls and swelling places. Did you mention me all day. How can I think in between. Henry McBride and Susan's pride. And plenty of chickens in every day. Oh how clean are lots of places.

I have thought very much about heat. When it is really hot one does not go about in the day-time. It is just as well to drink water and even to buy water if it is necessary. So many people diminish. And flowers oh how can flowers be north. They are in the air. How often do we air everything. Seem to me sing to me seem to me all safe. Seem to me sit for me sit to me all Wednesday. I do not mind July. I do not mind Thursday or Friday or Saturday. I do not mind breath of horses. We know what we think.

Give pleasure girls give pleasure to me and how do we know them in their turn. Because they do not turn away restlessly. We have imagined so much.

Amelia move Amelia move I can be recognized as that.

I can be seen by the light of the moon moonlight. I can be bright by my nephew's light, nephew contrite.

The nephew says, a marquise, a marquise if you please, she can read and write, and a willing, and willing to, willing to alight. Do not delude me by a beautiful word.

Can it be easily seen that country life makes us realise women giants and little negresses and the colour of curtains and almost always worth.

Can a planet please. Mildred is not pleased with the heat of the sun.

Johnny get your gun get your gun get your gun Johnny get your gun get your gun right off.

Johnny get your gun get your gun get your gun Johnny get your gun get your gun right off.

Mildred's thoughts are where. There with pear, with the pears and the stairs Mildred's thoughts are there with the pear with the stairs and the pears. Mildred be satisfied with tomatoes, apples, apricots, plums, and peaches, beets and ever greens, peas and potatoes. Mildred cares for us and Kitty Buss, what a fuss what a happy surprise. We only expected you last night and you have come again. When. It is very hot and no one knows what is the reason.

Can you think. Of me.

I have a sweet place full of air and of space. It is represented for me by idolatry. I idolise in this wise. When I am seated I am easily disturbed. When I love riches I am easily disturbed.

1922

84

IF HE THINKS: A NOVELETTE OF DESERTION

He was and is an, he was and is not named otherwise than Paul. Paul is his name and Paul is his character. Paul C. and Paul W. and Paul P. and Paul F.

In heaven very well oh very well and bees. He sees to them he seizes them and and Gabrielle may be a woman and is and is, she pleases and she is she is not married or the same. Can any one can any one does any one do they does he does Avignon.

Indeed no distress.

Indeed no mistress.

Indeed an old care.

Indeed they can care to see cousins and a brother. Cousins and a brother do not smother Avignon.

If he was freed.

Not at all.

His mother's debts.

Carrots hang on the wall.

And is that all.

Not at all.

They can have a pocket in a shawl.

And is that all

Not at all.

Paul.

In lamb and pork chops,

And mutton and beef roasts

In celery and spinach sauces

For boiled pears and prizes

And their mouths and their mouths, do not hesitate to sing by means of their mouths do not hesitate to hum by means of hives of bees painted regularly and put in under the trees.

She followed when no one followed. She was followed when no one was followed. She stood when no one stood she shrank when no one shrank, she mounted when no one mounted she settled when no one settled she did not crowd when no one crowded she did not draw when no one drew she did not announce when no one announced and she did not care to be bold to be told to scold not indeed to enfold. She did not care to be told, she did not care to

85

breathe it as air and why do you why did you go. I felt it necessary to go. Why do you go. I feel it necessary to go. Where to do go.

If in reading if in reading read to me. It is read to me. In this way a present and at present. He is present.

If Leontine is mine if she is he need not search for more any more.

Need not search for more any more.

If in walking, yes if in walking recognise walking as walking.

Recognise walking as walking.

How many stories are there in it.

INTERLUDE

Is this a surprise right in the middle of If he thinks thinks, I don't think I know why I love my baby so, she is rosy she is my posy she is so cosy she is so dozy little sweet complete my new year is my baby as a treat.

How many stories are there in it.

First.

London Paris Saint-Remy if he were three he would be free and he is three and he is free to gather what does he gather, he gathers as it were he does gather as it were he does gather and he meant to nourish me. Nourish and flourish are two necessary securities.

Can he say Paul.

Saul is another name.

Now as to a wife.

Now as to a wife in return.

Canals have water.

Canal water.

Canal water is used for irrigation.

Canal water flows and indeed it flows very well and runs and indeed it runs very [?well] and it overflows and it overruns and it is arranged for in a way it is arranged for and guns in this way guns are used and nearly in the evening and nearly not rapidly and very nearly not rapidly and they see when they look up into the tree they see very steadily they see and not he he does not see very steadily and yet not a defect. When is a defect not a defect when it is painstaking.

The history of Paul's measures and his active seas and no one sees more. More and more. How intentionally to revive.

Pillows, they call out and have sent, have sent for pillows. Pillows are used not used, pillows are used and they ask him to give them to them.

He does not expect to answer to-day. He does not expect them not to sleep at night. Night and bright. We are equally bright. And can you grieve Paul. Paul and grief and so are they often to cook little birds.

As well as huntsmen. Very well huntsmen. And travellers. Very well travellers. And tourists. Very well tourists. And ladies, very well ladies, and midnight masses very well masses.

If he thinks party for three.

We were very sorry for ease and grace and no Mabel not masses.

We were very sorry for easily and gracefully and no Michael not sheep. We were very sorry for accidentally and presently and no Nelly not knives. No nor can there be moments to more than Italians to more than balls to more than canals.

How do you think of canals.

Paul can do what Locker can do. Locker can do what Joseph can do. Joseph can do too what Arthur can do. And Arthur can do it all, he can readily restate changes.

Change again.

When this you see remember to be careful and not to deserve to have us say no no to-day yes yes to-day, we are going away, we are going away anyway.

He was not deluged with desertions and the son of an English mother and French father stayed. He stayed and his hand rested on a dog.

If in this way any one every one is obliging is obliged to satisfy whims and fancies, how prettily she seconds, and seconds, very many are more than seconds. I second and he seconds, and we second desertion and exertion.

A pronounced vocabulary.

Desertion and exertion.

If you do.

We did go away.

And we did come to you.

As an orator and an author as an author and as an orator and as an auditor and for sailors and fishes fishes and sauces, sauce for fishes and for meat and for meat and for cauliflower and not for potatoes nor indeed no nor indeed and for cheese and indeed and for oranges for indeed they came and for their shame and to their shame and with shame they name with shame we name with shame with shame with shame we name them so.

So they say.
He left to be gay.
Gay did you say.
He may forget.
Easily may.
And we.
We did say.
We were not to be assisted.
They were not to be assisted.
And another's son.
How often are apostrophes needed here.
A pronouncing dictionary of words for vegetables.
A pronouncing dictionary for words for butter and oil.
A pronouncing dictionary for words and vowels.
And so would anything else it would look like.

Does he say so does he say he too will be spared today. And he was he made a protest, it was the first time that he protested he had refused before but he had not protested, now he protested and had as result, not a choice but a change. A change and to change, a pronouncing vocabulary of sweets.

Unlikely more than likely.

I can easily place I can easily replace I can easily replace lace with lace.

To replace. Meadows and trees are cut down.

We have a pronouncing vocabulary of silver.

Silver cups silver in a cup, more silver and more settlements, more settlements and more satisfaction, more satisfaction and more unrest.

I feel that this is a vocabulary and I feel that there is a vocabulary of suspension bridges. We know of at least three varieties and we have very definite preferences. We prefer to cross them and recross them and we come across them.

Rhyme me with one of them. One of them and more than one of them. One of them out there.

I have lost interest in him. And you and you and you. We have lost interest in him. And you and you and you. We have lost interest in him as a captain of industry.

In finishing we say ram lamb sheep or mutton, mutton lamb sheep or ram, sheep ram lamb and mutton, mutton ram sheep or lam. When this is said everything is said. When everybody sings nobody sings. When nobody pleases. You please if you please he will not go so far readily and in anger. To finish.

1922

PROCESSION

Proceed to a procession.
The procession is prepared to proceed.
First procession.
In a procession.
And they were put opposite to us.
I turn.
If we turn if in carrying an animal its head is turned forward if a head of an animal is turned toward us does that affect the warmth of fur. Fur is very warm.
Nearly a procession.
A fable for a fact.
We like sheep and so do they.
They like them and he settles them there.
He likes it and so do they please themselves.
They feel that she misses her gold. Do you really, to be told. Do you mean that you are really told it told to be be told.
A procession forms by itself.
I se what you see. See me.

FIRST PROCESSION.

I proceed to sew.
We know.
We proceed to go.
And they know what they bestow. They bestow and it should be politely accepted anything that is given as free should be politely accepted.
They say so.

PART I.

They meant to seat themselves side by side and they tried not to do this beside not to seat themselves and not side by side. Beside what do they manage negroes a mother and a child.
We need hunters and we do not despair because in this country every one shoots. If every one shoots no one shoots. If everybody

hunts nobody hunts. Here everybody hunts and everybody shoots and everybody shoots and everybody hunts so you see it is not true that when everybody hunts nobody hunts. This is not true. Is it true for you. No it is not true.

First in a procession.

That is a beautiful procession and full of meaning too.

PART II.

In this way a procession they say.
Now and then.
Eating
A procession.
Lambing
A procession.
Penciling
A procession.
Cultivating
A procession.
Baking
A procession.
Familiarly meeting.
A procession.

PART III.

Hitherto a procession is not noisy.
And easily partial.
And very nearly practicable.
Please use practicable in this sense.

PART IV.

A part of part four is dedicated to this possession.

Part four may part may be a part may be a part because you see me because you did see me because of you.

Part four in part four around is round, and around around. She is around.

Part four.

To part for four.

Two part for four.

And those two and these two knew, they knew that they were necessary to oils and cheese. They knew they were necessary to oils and cheese.

They knew this and they do have pleasure in their weather. This does not plan and fan it. Not in winter nor indeed in summer nor indeed in spring nor indeed in the fall. Now we go and lose a ball. Not at all.

Carrots hang on the wall.

She can wear the shawl.

And is this all.

Not at all.

A procession is confusing.

PART V.

Plenty of time, plenty of time naturally.

PART VI.

Nearly a procession.

It was very nearly a procession. We proceeded to say so. And how do you know that the most softening moments in their life were as were stated.

They by this I mean not for them nor naturally not with them by this they mean why do you battle every may.

May we come to see an accusation. In this way a procession does not form itself in the character of an encircling of the town.

Let him see that they have mile posts centrally located. It is not at all certain that it is habitual to erect them here and there. If they succeed if they succeed one another, success has this title. I see them.

PART VII.

Indeed and indeed and indeed and may we and indeed see to it, that they need to proceed.

A procession forms at four.

A procession forms at five.

A procession forms at six.
A procession forms at seven.
A procession forms at four and five and six and seven.

PART VIII.

If they say I see them soon and they see me, then they say I will
address them soon and they will address me.
We do not live where we did.

PART IX.

Their part of the procession is the part that makes the procession
longer. Does it make the procession stronger. Longer and stronger.
Their part of the procession is the procession is the part that makes
the procession stronger and longer.

1923

IV
Plays

The two plays in this section fall within the last decade of Gertrude Stein's writing. Before this time she had experimented with many kinds of plays—the conversation play, the landscape play (movement in and out of a landscape) the portrait play, the opera. Four Saints in Three Acts, written in 1927, and set to music by Virgil Thomson, was performed for the first time in 1934 and was an immediate success. Gertrude Stein actually saw it performed in Chicago during her 1934-1935 trans-continental lecture tour. Plays of the last period tended to be melodramas or histories, culminating in Virgil Thomson's setting of The Mother of Us All, Stein's tribute to Susan B. Anthony and women's liberation.

"Daniel Webster" is a play made up of historical figures who did not actually overlap in historical time, but who do in Gertrude Stein's historical present. It has the timeless quality of a popular historical print by Currier and Ives. Nothing much happens, but some known and some unexpected relationships between the principal figures are played out. In one section, the curtain (the bane of Gertrude Stein's youthful theatre experience) is made to go up and down with curious frequency. Gertrude Stein achieves a great "operational" definition of pioneering: "'All who have ears have them clean and all who have doors have them open and all who have kitchens have them cooking. That is what pioneering is." "Daniel Webster" seems to be in some way, as an afterthought, related to Stein's novel Four in America in which she tried to tell what would have happened if Washington, Grant, Henry James and the Wright brothers had all done something quite different from what they actually did. In "Daniel Webster" everybody is himself again and the wives are along, too.

"Lucretia Borgia" is a play or an opera which seems to be a preparation piece for the later novel, Ida. It begins as a history but is soon lost in the pursuit of the twins Jenny and Winnie. The twins turn up later as Ida-Ida in Ida, and Winnie becomes the Duchess of Windsor caught up in the problems of publicity. As in all of Gertrude Stein's writing, history is now, and the content is the present. *Returned from her American lecture tour, Gertrude Stein was herself struggling with the problems of identity which publicity and eager audiences had put upon her. The killing of the twins seems to represent Gertrude Stein's attempt to get rid of the sense of audience which had, for a time, disturbed her writing. She does it in forty whacks: "one one one." The state of mind she preferred over identity was* entity, *and much of her later writing was done to recapture the innocence of this state of mind at the very time she had achieved her widest fame and audience.*

DANIEL WEBSTER. EIGHTEEN IN AMERICA: A PLAY

Four is a square.

A quarter section is a square of four.

ACT I

In a garden.

A garden in Missouri in Alabama in Concord in Norfolk a garden in Michigan.

Hiram   If anything is wanting in a garden water will help.

Ulysses   When I ate water in a garden it was when I saw four of them.

Suddenly Simpson came into the garden. As he came into the garden he knew Mrs. Simpson had come into a garden and Grant Grant never went into a garden he said, a garden has four walls.

A house near Saint Louis which does not have a garden.

George   George can always come into a garden and why not George can be anywhere. What is a George.

Washington   What is a Washington.

Wilbur   Wilbur can change.

Wright   Right right right left right I had a good job and I left right left.

Henry   There is no sister to a brother named Henry.

James   Oh yes all days are James.

All the characters having been now introduced he asks for Andrew Johnson and Andrew Johnson is dead.

SCENE II

A very large field in which in the winter horses make a round track and come in again.

Andrew Johnson has been there in the winter.

There is no difference between how old he is because nobody cares.

Grant Lincoln Webster and Calhoun take their places and Andrew Johnson is dead.

Webster Daniel Webster speaks, he is not interested in Andrew Johnson nor is anybody but nevertheless Daniel Webster speaks.

He says, if a father kills a brother is his son to be another. He says if a son kills a father will his father have a brother.

He says Daniel Webster says no one ever will kill Andrew Johnson because no one has any use for any one who is dead. Dead.

Daniel Webster speaks.

By which they tell that in that way no better silence can they pay. It is necessary that in their mentioning they should arouse that they go no farther and when they do that it should gather as it does whether they do rather hear them too. It is necessary, none then replied, it is necessary that when they take they put it away from them and from any of them. There is no one in any of them, they of necessity prepare not to divide.

Once more Webster speaks Daniel Webster speaks.

Speak when well spoken. The necessity of that which has grown diminishing and that which is diminishing reversing. In turning America back it can unwind. It is not necessity that no one does not allow for all of it. And so he says.

Daniel Webster speaks the last time.

Daniel Webster. When for the last time. Slowly Daniel Webster speaks when for the last time. Daniel Webster now has spoken he has spoken. Now for the last time.

As they move around all these who were there have forgotten Daniel Webster.

George Washington has forgotten him.

Grant has forgotten him.

Clay has forgotten him.

Wilbur Wright has forgotten him.

William James has not forgotten him.

Daniel Webster has spoken. He has said when for the last time his eyes shall see the stars and stripes the flag waving he hopes that he will not see it in two but that he will see it one and undivisible now and forever. That is what Daniel Webster says and Daniel Webster has spoken.

Is anybody listening.

No nobody is listening because Daniel Webster has spoken.

SCENE III

Here they come.
They are not in a garden.
They are not in a town.
They are not in the open.
Here they come.

SCENE III

When Daniel Webster knows that he knows that when for the last time he sees then the trap that was dug by one one for any one is the trap that that one does fall in. Daniel Webster knows.

And the Scene does not change and Daniel Webster knows. He knows.

All of a sudden they do not have to prepare they are all there. Daniel Webster knows that there is no all of a sudden. Daniel Webster knows. Daniel Webster knows that when he says for the last time it will not be for the last time.

Daniel Webster.   When for the last time.

And then they all come together as they stand.

SCENE IV

George Washington is George Daniel Webster is Daniel Webster Wilbur Wright is alright. Henry James is James.

And as they stand together they miss out one his name is Hiram Grant. They miss him out.

They look around and as they look around they miss him out.

George speaks.

Come say good-bye to me says George because good-bye is not so easy to say. Nothing is easy to say and so I say come and say good-bye to me.

Good-bye, George says good-bye. And as each one comes and says good-bye George says good-bye to him.

They do know some women their names are Martha or Elda or else Dolene and Irene.

George comes and not so carefully into the foreground.

None is with him.

He stands there anyway he stands there and he says.

I did say good-bye to every one of them one at a time.

97

That is what George Washington said as he was standing there.
He was standing.
George Washington stood.

Daniel Webster did not stand he moved and as he moved he did not remember George Washington. George Washington had not said good-bye to him.

SCENE IV

George Washington and Daniel Webster meet, they do not have to know one another.

They are both traveling but they are going in different directions but when they stopped for the night they stopped in the same place. There they were together and each one of them talked but not to one another. They did not know that the other one was there.

This is what each one of them said to those who were listening to each of them.

George Washington   Soap and Martha Washington.
Daniel Webster   Beware and with care.

A great many came upon the stage among them Wilbur Wright and Henry James and Hiram Grant. They do not see each other but they see that they are there.

They do not lean away together.

Each one speaks and Irene and Dolene and Martha and Mattie decide to be side by side and Abigail and Sarah have their place.

That makes a scene.

Mr. and Mrs. that makes a scene.

George Washington   To come is to say I have come.
Martha Washington   Away is where they go.
Daniel Webster   To go away is where they go. They go away, to-day when they go away.
Abigail   She makes it heaven to-day.
Mattie   I see Daniel Webster going away.
Abigail   Daniel Webster is not going away.
Daniel Webster   I knew along was long and about was gone and I knew where was left and that when was never lost and they engage to manage theirs best.
Daniel Webster   Thunder does not matter. Neither does lightning.

Abigail speaks to Mattie and Mattie speaks to Abigail.

What they speak they do not say.

Irene and Dolene come in with Wilbur Wright and Henry James.

Hiram Grant comes in. He does and does not look around. He speaks silently and he says. Once upon a time they needed to have girls come in girls and sons, once upon a time.

That is all he said.

Wilbur Wright did not say anything and then he began talking.

All that comes in comes in just as much as when you are not looking. Look again look so that it looks like the rest of them by the time by that time afterwards has no meaning not for me.

Wilbur Wright looked around.

What makes it be more pleasant, it is more pleasant.

Wilbur Wright arranges to go away.

Henry James   Buy fish.

Henry James sees Wilbur Wright preparing to go away and goes with him.

Henry James does not go with him.

After a while there are no people there.

SCENE V

The ground is there and Daniel Webster does not look around. As he travels he travels with George Washington and Wilbur Wright but not with any women. There are no women there. When he gets somewhere then there are women there Martha and Mattie and Abigail and Dolene and Irene. They are all sitting there. The men are together and the women are together they are talking and this is what they are saying.

Abigail   Mattie has come in.

Martha   I saw her come in

Irene   I saw Dolene and Abigail come in

Dolene   We have come in.

Daniel Webster does not commence to mutter he says very clearly I am coming here again.

Wilbur Wright says. In that case there is nothing to be said.

George Washington says, good-night.

Henry James says I am here.

Hiram Grant says I am here.

Daniel Webster says, If I am here then I will be here again.

And then they all go away either in or out and Abigail and Dolene finally go too. That is all.

They all come in again and then they are there.

99

George Washington was not asleep when Daniel Webster came in Daniel Webster did not see him but he spoke as if he spoke to to him. You are there Daniel Webster said to him. Yes George Washington said it again. He said yes.

Daniel Webster   There is no use in saying yes. say it again, I say there is no use in saying or having been saying and saying yes in saying what you are saying.

George Washington said yes again.

Irene and Dolene and Abigail and Martha and Henrietta were in the room together. They never looked around to see any one.

Wilbur Wright came in he spoke to them. He said. How do you feel do you feel pretty well do you all feel pretty well.

Each one of them said to him that they did they did feel pretty well.

Henry James was in the room but he did not come in. When he saw Wilbur Wright he did not come in. When he saw Daniel Webster he came in. When he saw George Washington he again did not come again. He said how do you do to each one of them. They each one of them said how do you do to him.

It is easy said one of them very easy and now there is not only Irene but there is Martha. Oh yes some are around oh yes there is Dolene. Yes there is Abigail and Henrietta and also Ida. Oh yes said one of them of course Ida is here.

Daniel Webster did not say that there was any difference between there and here.

George Washington said here.

Wilbur Wright said there.

Henry James said yes there.

After that they were all silent and thinking.

Irene and Martha and all the rest of them were thinking.

SCENE VII

Everybody who was able to be about was seated. It was not their habit to sit and so they were seated.

Each one after the other stood up, as they stood up and were not seated they all stood up. They did not stand up next to each other and pretty soon they sat down not all of them but some of them next to each other.

George Washington was not standing.

Daniel Webster was.

100

Wilbur Wright was.

Henry James was sitting and standing and Irene was sitting so was Dolene so was Martha and so was Abigail and Ida was standing and Henrietta was sitting.

Daniel Webster did not say anything but he looked around.

Hiran Grant came in, he saw Daniel Webster. He was the only one of them that said Daniel when he saw Daniel Webster.

He said Irene too when he saw Irene. Then he went away.

SCENE I

A garden in Alabama.

George Washington came in and some one was with him.

A garden in Connecticut.

Daniel Webster came in and Hiram Grant was with him.

A garden in Missouri.

Martha and Irene came in and Wilbur Wright was with them.

A garden in Michigan.

Abigail and Dolene came in and Henry James was with them.

Then they all sat down.

Hiram Grant was not among those present but he might have been. Daniel Webster might have spoken as if he might have been.

Daniel Webster never called them to open a door. He never called to them to open any door. No he did not.

Thank you Daniel Webster was never said to Daniel Webster.

SCENE II

There was a house but there was no garden in Indiana and Daniel Webster was never there but they knew about him.

He did not thank them for knowing about him much as he had heard it of them.

Out there in Indiana there was a house but not a garden.

Who came in

They came in

Who was in

They were in.

Not to begin

Begin is the same as began which is when they ran.

Daniel Webster did not run.

101

He could not win.
But Hiram Grant could
And so could George Washington.
This house which is not a garden is where they come.
They do not leave it nor do they go in.
Wait once at a time.
Yes wait once at a time.
And they have to go to stay.
George Washington does not stay away he never did but Abigail did and Dolene too, they stayed away.
Which was all that was necessary.
So then in Act One George Washington is seen when the curtain rises any one can see George Washington and any one can see when the curtain rises.
He can see Dolene and Abigail.
He can see Daniel Webster and Thoreau.
He can see Hiram Grant and Henry James.
He can see Irene and Wilbur Wright.
He can see Martha and George Washington.
And the curtain can come down and he can see them again.
The curtain can go up again.
Daniel Webster always has been.
Daniel Webster knows the difference between Daniel and Noah Webster and that is their religion.
Daniel Webster is there when the curtain goes up or comes down again. He is not waiting. He does not waiting while he is standing. He breathes again.
The curtain is going down and up and Daniel Webster is standing. He does not see Abigail or Irene or Dolene or Martha.

SCENE I

Yes well ink is better than water ink is better than water.
Daniel Webster turns around the other way just after he has said this.

Daniel Webster	If they are sleepy they will not go to sleep.
George Washington	She is asleep.
Abigail	Look at them.
Martha and Dolene	They do too sleep sitting.
Henrietta and Gabrielle	They look asleep but they are not.
Hiram Grant	Why not.

102

Nobody can answer.

Henry James   If not if not anybody can answer then indeed she is asleep sitting.

She supports her head upon her hand. Her eyes are closed. She had a warm coat on her and she awakes and then after then there is a little change in her position and she is asleep again.

Wilbur Wright   They can sleep with a hat upon their head.

Thoreau   A hat is never worn.

All together   If a hat is never worn then a hat is one.

SCENE II

It should be clearly stated that a name is not the same.

Daniel Webster never waited.

He did not.

If Daniel Webster never waited what did he do. He did what he did do and he never waited.

Any one of them all the same never waited.

It is no disappointment that no one ever waited. No one disappointed Daniel Webster. He was not disappointed.

Wilbur Wright   Wilbur Wright was disappointed.

Hiram Grant   Hiram Grant was not where disappointment is he was not no he was not.

Henry James might well have had what any disappointment can when it comes and when it goes. Henry James waited oh yes he did.

Thoreau   Thoreau oh oh did he know yes he did know that never here or there or anywhere where disappointment is and any where where there is and waiting is. As Thoreau waits. Well he waits.

George Washington made a song. He did not sing the song. He made a song of where he was when he was disappointed oh yes he was he made a song and the song was that song he waited and he was disappointed, not only disappointed but he waited.

And then all the women came and then all the women came. Muriel and then all the women came and Irene and Dolene and Martha and Abigail and they were not disappointed how could they they were not waiting how could they be disappointed they were not disappointed.

103

In the middle
They
Came to stay.
Even Daniel Webster.
Came to stay.
and if
Daniel Webster came to stay
They all
Stay.

George Washington Thoreau Daniel Webster Wilbur Wright Hiram Grant which is a mistake that is not his name and Henry James without a brother. The Jameses had both a father and a mother and so did Henry James. He can stay, that is because he does not have a brother. And once in a while he has not had a father and a mother. And George Washington answers when they ask him. So does Thoreau. Hiram Grant does not which is a mistake because he went away and did not come back. And Thoreau asked them to answer him and Wilbur Wright was quiet.

And then they did not see them come but they came Irene and Dolene and Abigail and Martha and Ellen and Isabel and Katherine and Jenny and Ida and Llewelen. When they came in.

Who then can say please run away not any who were there.
She thanked two of them three times.
Five came and when they came Daniel Webster was not there. He was never there when five came. He had a superstition that when five came he would not be there and he was not there. They came.
Daniel Webster was not there.
Henry James was there and when the five came they were all there George Washington and Noah Webster and Thoreau and Martha and Abigail and Dolene and Irene and Wilbur Wright and Hiram Grant they were all there. There is a mistake about that Hiram Grant had been there but he was not there but Ida was there and so was Netta oh yes she was.
And so five of them came in and they were all there and Daniel Webster was not there.

ACT II

Abigail was there.

Abigail called Dolene.

Was Abigail called Dolene or did she call Dolene.

Dolene was there.

Come here Irene and speak to Martha.

Come here Ida and stand behind Abigail.

Come here Ellen and arrange everything.

Wilbur Wright was not quiet.

He might have been dead but he was not quiet.

Henry James said he preferred that a curtain was quiet.

Then there was a storm the wind did not blow the clouds away. The hail came and there was no thunder at least George Washington had not heard any thunder and Hiram Grant did not see any lightning and Daniel Webster saw that a hole had been dug by the weather.

Martha and Abigail were not wet by the hail neither was Irene nor was Dolene Ida might have been.

After a very little time they called them away.

A dance when danced by a dog may mean that he is lonesome.

All who have ears have them clean all who have doors have them open and all who have kitchens have them cooking.

That is what pioneering is.

Daniel Webster has often spoken and as he has often spoken he has often told about what is open and shut.

In all their ears there are cheers.

But no one not Daniel Webster or any one can go where no one ever has been.

For which they thank.

Yes sir I thank you.

I thank you for what you have given.

And I will have pleasure in any undertaking which manages to cover nothing over or under.

Daniel Webster made many collect thunder. If they did they did know what rain is.

Come catch the rain if you can.

It is not often that many feel as they do about it.

Daniel Webster did not need a son or a daughter.

He had no desire for one or the other.

Neither one had a name. Noah Webster was not a brother.

And so they said, Daniel Webster Daniel was his name Daniel Webster said Remember whether any man is a brother remember a name remember the name that not any man is a brother because a brother if he does not live altogether can always kill not kill because nobody named Daniel can ever kill another.

When he said this there was a thrill. Some felt anxious and some gathered together. Who were they. Ah yes who were there.

Martin Martin was not a brother.

George George was not a brother

Wilbur was a brother but not his brother.

And Irene.

Who are sweetly Dolene can cry when anybody can say Irene.

Irene Oh yes Martha.

Irene Oh yes Abigail

Ida Oh yes Irene.

They came not into a garden but in summer, they came in the fall but not in the winter or in spring.

Daniel Webster was never seen in the summer. And why not. Because he had not a son or a brother or a daughter.

But Irene.

Irene had she said she had.

Come in dear Dolene.

Come in dear Abigail

Come in dear Irene.

And they all came in and it was spring and summer.

How are you they said as they came in.

George Washington did not complain of them nor did Henry James, Thoreau did but they did not listen and he told them excuse me. And as he said excuse me he remembered that his father that eminent man had known Daniel Webster.

Thank Daniel Webster for having know him.

Do you mind having been the son of Daniel Webster and if you do do you like all eight of them.

They refused to come together.

And one was Henry James.

Any one was Nelly Henry and any one was more often in in summer than in winter when they all had left.

In any scene they exercise not coming in.

Elmira and Isadora when they begin by that time they had not yet heard of California.

Daniel Webster never had arranged anything because or or they had no indifference.

Daniel Webster met no women. If he did he knew their name and he called them by that name. He remembered Dolene and Irene and Abigail and once or twice he was hoarse from speaking and he said I am speaking and he was.

This the way they came together. Who has lost his hat.

This is what he said.

If I have not lost my hat then the loss is nothing and Daniel Webster spoke again and enough were listening and he heard them listening. Speak again he said to them and he spoke again. Daniel Webster knew that Noah Webster was not his brother neither was George Washington or Thoreau or Wilbur Wright or Henry James or Hiram Grant.

It is a mistake Daniel Webster knew the mistake. Hiram was not his name.

Irene said I know all about his name.

And Dolene had violent eyes and she said I have heard him called Simon.

This again was not Daniel or David or even his.

Daniel Webster had never been interested in a king or in a queen and in no one in between. And this is what they said.

Dolene Irene Ida and Edith, Abigail and Henrietta, think well before you speak.

This is what Daniel Webster said.

They regret, think well before they regret.

No one interrupted any one they listened and Daniel Webster was waiting. He meant more than now. But now again not Daniel Webster never again not yet or again. Daniel Webster and again had no meaning and Daniel Webster said yes and when he said yes he did know that a flag was flying.

Daniel Webster   What is a flag.

There is no difference then Daniel Webster said it yet and again.

Thoreau and Dolene. They had a scene.

Hiram Grant never had nor could he have if he had spoken to Irene he could speak to Ida and he did speak to Dolene. When they all came together they sat and sang.

It was easy to sit and sing but did Daniel Webster do any such thing. Certainly he had sat and sung.

Now they are all in the house and there is an organ a little organ called a melodeon.

Thoreau and any one of them are standing and singing.

Now they do it again. Just as much again as anything.

Later on Daniel Webster and Hiram Grant never sang. Daniel Webster did not hear them sing Hiram Grant did hear them sing when they sang.

SCENE II

Dolene and Irene sitting together while they sing.

Daniel Webster is listening.

George Washington is standing.

Henry James is wistful and he is watching, he is neither sitting nor standing and Abigail is speaking to him she speaks to him and as he listens she does not go on speaking. Once in a while Martha Washington can and does come in.

Now listen.

Daniel Webster never asked any one who knows my name why did he, he did not.

George Washington had said nothing when Daniel Webster had not asked him. No he did not say anything then and he did not say anything later. He very often said something but he did not say anything then.

Dolene and Irene listened they listened to each one of them and then they listened to them.

Daniel Webster. He never called Irene to him but he did call Dolene.

George Washington did not he did not call Irene and he did not call Dolene not to him.

Abigail listened and then she came not slowly not at all not when she did not come but she came. Abigail was her name.

William James was seated he naturally preferred sitting to standing but Wilbur Wright not. This was not necessary that Wilbur Wright did. Who did.

Thoreau. Thoreau spoke to Daniel and then he spoke to Noah Webster and then he spoke to Hiram Grant. He spoke in a low tone he spoke to them.

108

I am happy to see you he said to each one of them.

Abigail heard him but that was natural it was natural that Abigail heard him.

Are you coming said Henrietta and Ida and everybody answered them. They did not listen but they heard that everybody was answering them and then they went away.

They all said that they preferred that a garden should have a picket fence after all it was better to have one and everybody said it was better to have one. Thoreau spoke again. He said I am speaking and he was he was saying that he was speaking to several of them and he was.

SCENE IV

Later in the day it was not sunset yet. It never could be sunset because the sun did not set. One of them came in.

Nobody looked at him. He was there and they did not care to hesitate but he hesitated about coming in. Irene and Dolene never had thanked him and he said his name was William.

No one knew him.

He said I like what I am doing.

Daniel Webster had gone away and Noah Webster was counting. Abigail came in to go out again and Ida said it was better to stay than to go away and she told William to stay. William had not gone away.

Thoreau came in again and when he saw William he came in again.

How are you said Thoreau to William. William was looking at George Washington.

Henry James did not see William but Ida did and so did Martha. Dolene and Irene went away not into the garden but into another room.

They could not be careful about that, they could.

Come in said William.

Thoreau mentioned that he had seen Hiram Grant.

How old is he said Thoreau.

After that George Washington said good-day and went away, he rode away.

Daniel Webster did not thank you one.

All of a sudden there they all were again. Oh yes they were.

Even if they had not been there they were. They had not all come in again but they were all there and they would come in again

109

and there they were. They spoke to each other saying it is time to come in.

Daniel Webster said, he was reciting, he said he dug a pit he dug it deep he dug it for his brother, into the pit he did fall in the pit he dug for tother. They heard him recite this thing. They did not all listen as they heard him recite this thing. They did not all listen as they heard him recite this thing but he did recite this thing.

Any one can not come again.

Not any one who can not come again can not come.

Who came.

George Washington had been

Wilbur Wright came.

Dolene came.

Not Irene.

Thoreau had not been

Henry James was standing.

Abigail and Martha had stopped leaning.

Daniel Webster did not see Noah Webster, Noah Webster had come.

Daniel Webster was not reciting nor was he listening. Once in a while they can and cannot come.

Who came in

Hiram Grant did not come.

Ida and Henrietta can come.

They need not necessarily be quiet because they do not talk.

Daniel Webster never had mentioned a thousand not a thousand thanks not a thousand words not a thousand.

After all no thousand.

Any nobody said how do you do.

They did of course but nobody said how do you do.

This Noah Webster knew, he knew that they did and he knew that a thousand was a hundred times ten and ten was ten times one, Noah Webster knew everything.

And that is what nobody said.

Come again said Noah Webster to all of them.

Daniel Webster was dead.

He had not gone, he was after all all ready to come again.

Nobody was waiting.

He did not go away.

Who heard anybody.

Nobody heard anybody.

Noah and Daniel eat together

110

Somebody said they do not know each other.

And Dolene and Irene were very often there where everybody said that Noah and Daniel had not met.

Dolene said not yet.

And Irene said yes.

Abigail said she had always preferred yes to yet

And Martha and Henrietta and Ida were there.

Of course they were there.

Abigail had heard from them that they were there

George Washington turned his back on a fountain.

Wilbur Wright came and looked at a mountain

And Henry James as he came in was humming.

Thoreau asked him what he was humming.

And Henry James answered him and said he was humming a song.

Thoreau asked him what was the song he was humming.

And Henry James said that he would like very much like to tell him.

Dolene and Irene came in.

When they saw them Dolene came in and Irene came in

They need not expect that any one who had gone away had gone away to stay.

They felt better then

ACT III

SCENE I

It is when they come in that they feel at home. Daniel Webster spoke to them.

Daniel Webster said it was a hen.

Nobody answered him.

He said. When

Nobody answered him.

He said moreover I will never acknowledge that it is better to judge five than ten.

George Washington answered him. He said it is very well very well that it is better to judge five than ten.

Daniel Webster did not begin again he was not there when they went in again.

111

He said when do they go away again and everybody answered him. They said they could not go as they were there to stay.

Daniel Webster did not answer them.

Thoreau said that he had heard that there were more there when there were five than when there were ten.

Everybody answered him. They said to him that they had not heard what he had said, and he thanked them.

Wilbur Wright was not frightened he said that it was all right that he was never frightened that he had a brother and that that brother was not there but he said that he was not frightened.

Henry James said that he was there.

Irene was very pleased to hear him say this thing. Dolene helped her and then together they were pleased that he had said it then.

Hiram Grant was very often there but he did not say that he had it to do. Not yet or more than ever. No one heard him and Abigail and Martha and Henrietta were furious they said that everything was better. And it was.

Daniel Webster   Oh yes, they said oh yes.

Daniel Webster   Daniel Webster said yes.

SCENE II

Act III does take place Daniel Webster knew very well that Act III does take place and so he takes the place of Act V

During Act III he arouses every one who come in and as they come in they are aroused.

If they are aroused no one can say I meant or I mean all they can do is to be aroused and as they are aroused they are there. Oh yes there where no one did know one from another. Daniel Webster oh Daniel Webster who can measure the Daniel in Daniel Webster. That is what no one says but as no one says Daniel Webster is there and he is altogether there altogether so there can be a length to Act III

George Washington will remember that Daniel Webster will remember that Daniel Webster.

For once there is no silence.

George Washington will remember that Daniel Webster did not only arouse every one that Daniel Webster was there and George Washington did remember so did William Dean, oh yes William Dean how did you come in. Nobody had seen George Washington and William Dean had come in he was with him and George Washington had not come in and so where was Daniel Webster he was not only not there but not again.

Oh thank you said William Dean it was a pleasure to have seen him and a pleasure to hear him. Daniel Webster is speaking.

SCENE IV

It takes a whole scene and Daniel Webster although he is standing looks like sitting like a sitting man. He begins speaking.

When I was coming they came and they saw that all were coming and they all were coming and in a little while as they all saw and saw that they were all coming I looked away from them.

This is what Daniel Webster said.

And then he had not stopped and so he went on.

As they were seen they could not tell which one had been looking, how could they come to see that no one had been looking since each and every one were going on coming and then just then it was not loud it was out loud, out loud, out-lawed, out and not allowed, allowed, no one can see any one who is not the one no one can have come if and of course he is that one that one not allowed, out-lawed, out-lawed, yes out loud.

Listen, and they listened to him, listen, no less listen.

Then Daniel Webster was speaking and now he was looking not like a man sitting he was looking like a man standing.

SCENE I

Who has broken a house, who has hoped that wood is made useless by cement and stones made useless by water and widening made useless by pails of water and horses that carry water. Who has made them call them and as they call them who has asked them to widen a river. Who has. Who can answer when they know the dog is eight years older and therefore had no further interest in watching sheep, who can say aloud what he has heard when they do not compare water with water who can call them when they have been thoughtful about how often they met frenchmen, who can be left as a test a test of welcome, who can be careful that they could not ride horses, and after all to come again.

George Washington heard them when they said everything and Grant heard them when they said everything and Thoreau did Thoreau hear them.

Daniel Webster believe Daniel Webster believe him.

Daniel Webster when he speaks does not speak of snakes although he had often seen them real snakes snakes that were snakes and if they did not rattle could at the same time sting any one but as almost every one wore high boots then they did not sting them the snakes did not even when they struck at them. This was not what Daniel Webster said but it was what Daniel Webster knew and all the others knew this too all all of them. All of them.

Daniel Webster   When indeed and at best and when moreover they do not need what they have they do not need rest then all of them.

Interruptions begun and ended by all of them.

Daniel Webster   And when morever they need to allow that they need never share what no one has to consider a care when they remember that care and consider are the two words which are welcome then all of them.

Once more all of them commence interrupting they gather themselves together until they are all together and then they say we have not begun not begun and they say no not begun and all of them all of them have not begun.

Daniel Webster   When indeed there shall be the exchange between what they need and on what they feed when it shall moreover never be necessary that all of them.

All of them knocking something over keep calling all of them all of them all of them.

Daniel Webster   When there is authority when they have to have no one in authority when they outline where there is no outline what do they have within what have all of them what have they within what have they within all of them I say all of them what is within within all of them.

And all of them did not answer him they were not there then no not there not all of them none of all of them were there they were not hiding they were where they had not been they were not there not any one of all of them not any of them.

Daniel Webster went on speaking George Washington heard him and so did Henry James and Wilbur Wright and Parkman. Then one at a time they heard him and Daniel Webster went on speaking he did not speak to them he said. Once when I was present I was present not as I had been but as I am I am present and as I am present once when I am present I speak of that thing.

And they all listened to him.

114

Daniel Webster went on speaking. Once when George Washington met Washington Irving what did he say to him Daniel Webster did not answer himself and he did not stop standing but he did stop speaking.

ACT THE ONE BEFORE THE LAST

SCENE I

Daniel Webster believed that thunder followed lightning and he said so. As he said so there was lightning and as he said so there was thunder and as he said so the thunder followed the lightning they all heard him. Come again they said to him and as he had not left them he did not answer.

Please ask him said Wilbur Wright and Henry James said I am asking him and George Washington said it is very often certain that thunder does follow the lightning. Everybody everybody who had been there Martha Washington and everybody who had been there everybody heard him when he said this thing.

ACT I

This is the last Act

SCENE I

Daniel Webster knew he had a country. He knew it.

Daniel Webster. Nobody knows that neither he knows or either they know or either they will know, nobody knows and when the moon rose nobody knows nobody will know that there is no matter, no matter the only one that matters is George Washington and I said Daniel Webster I, do not see him. This is what Daniel Webster said. George Washington was there standing before him and Wilbur Wright and Thoreau and Henry James and William Grant and Thoreau and Ulysses Simpson Grant there they all stood and some of them were talking and Martha Washington and every one were always sitting and some of them said something like that and no one saw Daniel Webster Daniel Webster was there and nobody saw him standing, he was not standing he was sitting.

115

Daniel Webster   Anybody who has seen a man and his country.

Remember said Daniel Webster everybody who has seen anybody and the flag of his country.

George Washington was not silent that is to say he did not say anything and Martha Washington came with him that is to say came with him.

Henry James met Mildred, Mildred had just lost a tooth and that did not make her nervous because it had come out naturally and Thoreau knew Adelina and meant to go away with her but she left all alone and that did not matter. And Wilbur Wright mentioned that he had a sister and this sister was named Eva Simon Guise and Wilbur Wright wished that he had known her but he had left home before she was his sister or long before she was his sister and now she was sitting and Daniel Webster was standing with her and Hiram Grant said that no one who knew Daniel Webster would either like to go away or not, he never did. Just then Daniel Webster sat down.

Daniel Webster said that there was no difference between summer and winter in either one he could smell cooking if they were cooking and in summer and in winter they would be cooking something. This never made Daniel Webster nervous, not exactly, he liked everything they cooked and when he ate he would stop to listen, to listen to what he would say if he were not then eating what they had been cooking. This is what made him a companion to George and Martha Washington and Martha Washington mentioned it when she said it to George Washington and George Washington mentioned it when he spoke to Daniel Webster and this is what they said.

Who knows said George Washington and this is what he was saying who knows what it is that Daniel Webster said, I do said George Washington and everybody listened to him. And then George Washington went on talking, listen to me he said and I will tell you what Daniel Webster said and Thoreau said and Henry James said and Wilbur Wright and Ulysses Grant said, you will be listening to what they said when I tell you what they said, this is what George Washington said and Martha Washington nodded her head and they all either sat or stood and George Washington went on talking.

Buy a principal Daniel Webster said Daniel Webster no less a principle than a practice.

Daniel Webster aroused Daniel Webster.

Finally they said in fact finally they said and Daniel Webster. Daniel Webster   Can they in their case stand and fight can they in their case mean and neglect can they can they in their case follow and turn can they can they can they not can they be having it for more than a circumstance of their knowing which they wore and is cloth woven and for which in which circumstance. Sheep not dogs have wool. But said Daniel Webster some dogs resemble sheep insofar as they seem to have wool. Daniel Webster dreamed he dreamed of awaking and as he awoke he spoke.

Daniel Webster might be generous in spots and if he is he is he says spots what are spots are here and there and all over and that is what makes a leopard. Spots make a leopard and shares shares are very plenty.

Why said Daniel Webster why is money money, money is not money when it is owed to yourself and that is what makes a country bankrupt, bankrupt, bankrupt said Daniel Webster because money is only owed to themselves not to another. George Washington knew about money so did Henry James but so did Thoreau, Wilbur Wright no and Martha Washington and many another no. And so.

Daniel Webster went on. If there is no one here who is another, not any one here who is any other then if there is no one to whom you owe how can you be bankrupt so there no so, a child cannot be convicted of stealing from its parents oh no, the french say so, Daniel Webster said they could not but they can and they do and they do not Daniel Webster said so.

And so it happens that is what it is and so gradually nothing is said more than so.

SCENE II

Daniel Webster went on

The End.

1937

LUCRETIA BORGIA. A PLAY

For a while Lucretia Borgia was hurt because she had no cousins. She would have liked to have cousins. Then she suddenly said, he knows, and when she said he knows she meant my lord the duke. The duke was cut off by his position from listening and every little while he liked to be patient, they were after all happy together dear duke and dear Lucretia Borgia but not really very often.

LUCRETIA BORGIA

A PLAY

5 characters and a crowd, a house, a hill and a moon

ACT ONE

Hands open to receive and to give. Lucretia had a house a hill and a moon, she had had to see why she was not early to bed. Gentle Lucretia. What was the trouble. What was it she said. She said that Lucretias are often very nicely received by everybody, and why not, when all a moon does is to stare. Alright. Forget it. This is the first act of Lucretia Borgia.

Lucretia Borgia

Be careful of eights.
Lucretia's name has eight letters in it, do be careful of eights. With Winnie and Jenny one does not have to be so particular.
But with the name Lucretia, it is unpardonable not to be careful with the name Lucretia Borgia quite unpardonable.

Lucretia Borgia.

LUCRETIA BORGIA

AN OPERA

ACT I

Lucretia's name was Gloria and her brother's name was Wake William. They kept calling to each other Gloria Wake William.

And little by little the name stuck to her the name Gloria, really her name was Lucretia Borgia when it was not Jenny or Winnie. How useful names are. Thank you robin, kind robin.

LUCRETIA BORGIA

ACT I

Lucretia's name was Jenny, and her sister's name was Winnie. She did not have any sisters.

Lucretia's name was Jenny that is the best thing to do.

Jenny's twin was Winnie and that was the best thing to do.

LUCRETIA BORGIA

ACT I

Jenny was a twin. That is she made herself one.

Jenny like Jenny liked Jenny did not like Jenny

So then Jenny said Winnie.

It is wonderful when Jenny says Winnie.

It just is.

Winnie oh Winnie. Then she said and they all looked just like Winnie.

PART II

Jenny began to sit and write.

Lucretia Borgia—an opera.

ACT I

They called her a suicide blonde because she dyed her own hair.

They called her a murderess because she killed her twin whom she first made come.

If you made her can you kill her.

One one one.

1938

V
Literary Music

In the Primer *I illustrated how the work Gertrude Stein did in the 1920s was a consolidation of the change of style of the 1912 or "Spanish Period" and the romantic 1922 or "San Remy Period." This new period of gentle playfulness I called a kind of concentrated literary "chamber music." Portraits were done in this new style, plays were done in this style, geography, poetry and narration. Key works of the time were* Composition as Explanation *(1926),* Useful Knowledge *(1928) and* An Acquaintance with Description *(1926).*

After so much romantic emotion, a more formal and analytical note is struck again. Themes related to mathematical thinking are chosen and elaborated: numbers, counting, propositions, parts and wholes, demonstrations, geometrical configurations, measurements, volumes, problems and enclosed, measurable spaces.

"Studies in Conversation" begins with a dialogue as exact as musical scales being practiced to a metronome. After the warm up, the piece begins: "Practicing, practice makes perfect." Themes are stated, varied, developed. There are arpeggios of being and buying, following and hurrying. There are contrasts of asleep and awake, no and yes, god-father and god-mother. There are extensions of cake to awake, meant to sent, thought to sought. The writer's inner voice reminds her to "Describe it continuingly and not as a forethought." No past or future, only the continuous present.

In "Are There Arithmetics," "How large is a field when fenced" presents the problem. Around this problem the mind plays in language freed from stereotyped thought. The problem is considered in parts, it is stated, it is made very plain, it is quantified ("how many are there how many are there"), it is repeated, it is nearly finished. Language is denotative and measures out the meaningful relationships with a sense of order and precision.

"Made a Mile Away" is organized around a list of painters or paintings that remain vital and present to the writer—Millet, Botticelli, Tintoretto, El Greco, Gauguin, Cezanne, Matisse and Picasso: "Among the influences which made me what I am." Some pictures are described: "The first thing that is to be noticed is grey and

green. *The next thing to be noticed is green and blue—." Finally what attracts Gertrude Stein's attention is not pictures* per se, *but the inner content of direct, moment to moment description, unrelated to the scheme of the piece. She ends making her own picture in words. Subject and object are one.*

"Descriptions of Literature" is an ingenious inventory of the books in Gertrude Stein's immediate interior or exterior environment. There are over sixty of them, each with its delicious individualistic flavor. The composition proceeds as a list, a common form for the writer at this time. The description proceeds by declarative statements. Some are believable summaries: "A book which attracts attention." Other propositions are harder: "A book describing six and six and six." All are no doubt literal judgements, spontaneously made in successive creative moments.

"Five Words in a Line" is as tightly composed as a Bach fugue. It begins in measured cadence: "Five Words in a Line." This is varied, extended, negated, interrupted, found again and withheld. A second section introduces new themes about people: "They look at him and they know what he thinks." These themes are varied, but we then "come back" to "Five Words in a Line . . ." and a grand cadence of resolution at the end: "By never being suspicious and always being careful she has never been robbed." All the pieces in this section reflect the mind in nimble, formal play.

STUDIES IN CONVERSATION

One—   Are there six.
Two—   Or another question
One—   Are there six
Two—   Or another question.
Two—   Are there six.
One—   Or another question.
Two—   Are there six.
Two—   Or another question.

As studies in conversation.

Studied.

Practicing, practice makes perfect. Practicing, perfect, practicing to make it perfect. Practice, perfect, practice. As perfect. Practice. Perfect. Practice.

Introducing practicing introducing practicing, practicing, introducing, practice introducing. Introducing practicing. Practicing introducing.

Not at all.

When there is no reason for it, when is there no reason for it. When there is no reason for it. When is there a reason for it. It is not needed at all. It was not as it was not, as it was not, no need to cry and no need to cry. It was there that and have it for that. In decision.

Opposite to it, as it is opposite to it, for it, for it and opposite to it, opposite to it and for it, for it, opposite to it, opposite to it, for it.

Before it, before it and in respect to it respect for it, and in respect to it, before it and before it, before it is begun. And before it is begun and seconds.

Assist her. Assist her or to assist. Ought to assist ought she to assist. Ought she to assist her. Ought she to assist, assist her. So nearly buying, so nearly living, so nearly seeing, so nearly being, so nearly being buying, so nearly being or nearly buying or so nearly, or so nearly buying, seeing, or so nearly seeing buying. She was so nearly seeing buying.

Might it be occasionally might it occasionally be sooner, might it be as soon, might it be occasionally as soon might it be as occasionally as that and might it be might there be an occasion, might there be this occasion for it. Was it nearly mine.

What.

What fell.

It is remarkable remarkably noticeably remarkable that when we hesitate we make a decision eventually. So much for that. And moreover a great many there are a great many instances of it. So questioningly.

Another no, no no, yes, as yes, it is as yes that she speaks, she speaks it is as yes as yes that as yes that she speaks. It is as she speaks.

After, find her, find her afterwards. Afterwards find her. Afterwards and find her.

Weeks for weeks. A week and for a week. In a week.

No notion of what it is.

More than once.

Not, not asleep.

Honey cake as awake.

Borders borders to a lake borders of a lake the borders of a lake are those which the border of the lake is the border which does not unquestionably present itself. And so most often.

Interestingly.

Describe it continuingly and not as a forethought. Forethoughtfully or thought, or thought or sought.

And why do they settle as hers. So need he.

In a little and they can can they and in so much.

Much much much. Coated. And they can can they and in so much.

Any way.

A new violet.

As opposed to it.

Fancy and fancying.

If what is worn and made is made, if seating and seated are serious and they said that, if in no case and kept carefully not at all as a gift.

If a thing has existed for a certain length of time it is not newly inaugurated.

So many.

And so many.

And follow in this way.

Have to hurry.

They have to hurry.

They have to hurry to follow in this way.

It says so.

As it says so.

What do they put in it.

I hear you.

As pieces.

A piece of it.

What were the causes of the pleasure they took in it.

The first cause of the pleasure they took in it the real cause of the pleasure they took in it was their reason. Their reason is that nearly as much so as can be has been for and against wishes. Meanwhile, in the meantime not unreasonably very many say so, have it variably, if in their way if it is in their way. So much better, it is so much better that there has been an instance of it.

So nearly precisely carried carefully and no more.

What was meant when they sent it to us, this to us what was meant when this was sent when it was sent to us, what was meant when it was sent, it was sent to us.

A god-mother to her her god-mother. A god-father to him, his god-father. A god-father a god-mother, her god-mother his god-father, his god-mother her god-father, her god-mother his god-father. So and so. So and so is his god-father. And so her god-mother, as god-mother. God-mother to whom and when.

This is the question, if the potato which grew in that way and in that place and was bought from them and sold here, would it if there was reason to explain it any way would the explanation be more than eminently satisfactory to one and not to the other. Not to one and not to the other. In the same way about fish and presents. Would an explanation which was completely satisfactory commit any one altogether. Would it give pleasure. Would it mean that to all of those who believe sincerely believe that as one rises and as one as two as three as four and no more. And really not any more. Not any more. Why as much more. Why is there so much more day-light. This is only because each likes that shape their shape for themselves.

1923

ARE THERE ARITHMETICS

Are there arithmetics. In part are there arithmetics. There are in part, there are arithmetics in part.

Are there arithmetics.

In part.

Another example.

Are there arithmetics.

In part.

As there are arithmetics. In part.

As a part.

Under.

As apart.

Under.

This makes.

Irresistible.

Resisted.

This makes irresistible resisted. Resisted as it makes.

First one to be noticed.

Another one noticed.

To be noticed.

The first one to be noticed.

First one to have been noticed.

Are there arithmetics, irresistible, a part.

Are there arithmetics irrestible resisted a part.

Are there arithmetics irresistible apart.

Ever say ever see, as ever see, ever say.

Notably.

Arithmetics.

Are there arithmetics, a part.

Bowing and if finished.

Are there arithmetics a part.

Ever say.

Are there arithmetics if finished, bowing if finished are there arithmetics ever say, are there arithmetics apart.

Not four.

No sense in no sense innocence of what of not and what of delight. In no sense innocence in no sense and what in delight and not, in no sense innocence in no sense no sense what, in no sense and delight, and in no sense and delight and not in no sense and delight and not, no sense in no sense innocence and delight.

Alright.

Don't you think it would go into arithmetic nicely.

If and intend if and intend, if and to attend, if and if to attend if to attend if and intend, or and nearly equal, two ahead and four behind, two ahead and two behind, two ahead as two, and two, and two ahead and have to, and have it or in needles in case of.

I am not sure I like that one there are arithmetic one day.

If in it as if in it as as has if in it as it has if in it as it has been, if it has been as if it had had as if it had had it as it was, as it were if it were to be captivated, if it were in this and that way very fairly stated, state it. To state it.

Gradually in counting as gradually as counting. If there are more.

Now see here.

Plain plain plain. To be plain, it is plain it is made very plain, plainly. And arithmetic and more so, and more or so. Grapes and chocolate. Name it flourish to flourish to flower, name it as flower or flourish or name it as flourish as flower or flower.

How large is a field when fenced. How many are there of hats and hats, how many are there of cows and cows how many are there how many are there are there many and how many and who says so, so and so.

Now repeat it. Can I repeat it. I can repeat it. As I repeat it, as I repeat it, they and they do, do and do do, do and do too, do and do do. As to a shot, and as to a shot and as to and as as to a shot, a shot or anyway they and to-day very industriously the nearly finished.

It had no intention, it as it had it and it it had no intention, Dora Katorza and it had no intention it had no intention.

Or or or will they plunge us into or, or or or will they will they will they or, or or or will they plunge or will they, they will not. What, rice, what rice or what pears or or what rice or what or not, pears rice, will they or will they not. And what do they mean. They mean to keep by this they mean to keep it or by this means by this means they mean to keep it. Or or or do they mean to bring some more.

Double cover and a double cover. Double cover a double cover. Double cover. A double cover. Double cover. A double cover is used when the one and the double cover is used not used up. The double cover. A double cover and a double cover. Cover.

Shove her.

Not a knee not a knee, see knee. Not a knee not a knee see me. Knot a knee not knot a knee to me.

So Mike did.

In funny too funny, too funny for funny for funny as funny as funny is funny. Is funny. It is funny.

Be can be back, be can be back. For this because of this reduplication.

Arithmetic or more. Cora Moore. They cannot forget interesting days.

Nice little new little new little nice little nice little new little three. New little nice little nice little new little new little new little as three. Three. Three. Then seated. Then sit as if to be seated. I newly carried I carried it away.

Why and why, why and why, not nearly astonished enough.

1923

MADE A MILE AWAY

Made a mile away.

Description of all the pictures that have attracted some attention.

First Millet. Several miles away or a description.

Juan and Juanita.

First Millet. Thirty miles away as thirty miles away.

Juan and Juanita very differently in a place.

As to places.

Millet as to places.

Juan and Juanita and not as to places.

Millet so much.

Millet so much.

Millet so much Millet so much.

Juan and Juanita for the sake of measure. To measure a settler safely. Juan and Juanita in the past time.

And caring.

Millet has no other father has no other sister has no other either. Millet has no other or either as he has no other. As he has no other.

Juan and Juanita establishes. Juan and Juanita establishes grain and furs and less and silver and as you call and as you call it and so very much and as much and meaning and in enterprise and for a place and finally and as it has.

As much of it.

A second case there is a second case, there is in case of it.

Botticelli makes more uncles for no reason.

So much for sewing. It is as much as that. It is as much as that. And so much. So much so. So much for sewing. It is as much as that so much for sewing.

To remain and happily to do so this is in memory of having it as it as it has it. This is in the memory of only here and there. So much so.

The next was Tintoretto and asleep. Tintoretto and asleep Tintoretto Tintoretto Tintoretto and asleep Tintoretto for if for all if free for all if as far as as far as that. It is not as far as that now. Why. Because there is no use because it is in use, because it is usually, usually how usually, as usually. And so forth.

The next was not more so.

The next was not more so and as much so. Giving it a name all the same. Harry, giving it a name all the same. Not Harry and not giving it a name all the same. Not Harry and not Harry and, and giving, Harry giving it a name, not Harry and not giving it a name all the same.

Next, El Greco. Found by itself as if it were as if it was, it was, it was found by itself and not so for so and as so as so much. Longer so much longer and so much. So much longer and so much and Anthony and so much. So much so and so much. Anthony and as not so much longer. So much longer and seen, feel seen fell seen, fell saw saw it saw him, saw him sell him, see him, seen. As seen a scene. So and seen, seen so, seen as as much longer and seen as so much and as seen and so long. Not good-bye but so long. Longhi. Very nice and quiet I thank you.

Next next is next was the next was the one with as sitting one as sitting two as sitting three as sitting, three as sitting all three as sitting and in this way as a lap, in this way sitting as a lap, in this way all three all three as this way, Anne as this way Mary as this way, all three as this way sitting as this way, this way as sitting and in itself to itself so itself as in as on and as on and as in, and so as pleased now. Have it the same. Do have it the same. Have it the same can have it the same. Have it the same as nearly.

Next. How next.

If I see to see if I see you see, if you see to see, if to see you see, as you see have it to see, have it to see you see. You see Courbet and it is so resembling. It so resembles it resembles it so, it resembles it so much. As much. As much as that. It resembles it as much as that. This as this so much this as this, as that so much this as this, this as that, so much this as that, this as this. So much as this. So much as this. Newly.

Newly or newly and newly and newly, and newly and newly. Newly too.

Which when they do.

Have it or refuse to have it or have it or not to refuse to have it, or have it, have it, a question, have it, to question, to have it, have it, have it now. And to have to now. Also.

Extra changes many doors and mixed as across.

Felt indeed indeed felt it was indeed felt it was felt it was indeed it was felt and so in, principally having more nearly fluttered.

Next time looking. Looking means more. Next time and looking and looking means more. Mention Gauguin. If there and Greuze, mention Gauguin if three and Greuze and mention Gauguin and if three and if Greuze and if mention Gauguin and if there and if mention and if mention Greuze and if to mention

131

Greuze. If there and if Gaugin and if to mention and if Greuze. If there if and if there and if to mention.

Greuze if to mention if three and if to mention Gauguin and if to mention Greuze and if there and if Gauguin and if to mention Gauguin and if to mention Greuze and if three. If three and if to mention and if Greuze if there and if to mention and if Gauguin and if to mention and if three and if Greuze. If three and if Greuze if three and if to mention. If Gauguin and if to mention. If to mention and if there and if to mention.

Payed unpayed payed. Unpayed unpayed unpayed payed. Paid to see it paid to see Cezanne. Whom did it pay. Pay him oh yes pay him, paid him oh yes paid him, paid him oh yes paid him paid him oh yes.

Fancy for that.

To have a fancy for that.

Next.

Next and left.

Left.

Left right left.

Left right left he had a good job and he left, left, left right left.

Next one and one and one make three.

The next was was it.

The next was the next was was it.

Coming back to coming back to back.

If Cæsar if Cezanne if Louis if later, if Henry if in favour if in favour if fairer if no fairer than that if no further and then it is strange that it is not any stranger at all.

This was the effect of it.

If Henry.

Henry was and Henry. Henry was and Henry and so forth.

The effect of Henry was the effect of Henry was on me.

When this you see remember me.

The effect of Henry was on me.

Henry Matisse for instance.

For instance Henry Matisse. No decision.

For instance Henry Matisse and no decision.

For instance.

Henry Matisse.

For instance.

No.

For instance.

Decision.

For instance Henry Matisse and effect on me.
Effect on me.
For instance.
Henry Matisse.
Lo the poor Indian and so forth.
For instance.
Next.
Next.
I had.
Next.
Next.
I had a good job.
Next Next.
I had a good job and I.
Next.
Next.
I had a good and I left.
Seriously speaking seriously speaking I described, seriously speaking seriously speaking I described, seriously speaking I described seriously speaking.

What picture do I have after, what picture do I have afterwards.

What did I notice after I noticed after I did notice, what did I notice after I did notice it.

First, firstly, at first, and first, first and first, first and first and longer, at first and at first and longer longer as long, as long as that.

This changes this changes that. If in choosing choose one and two if in choosing to choose one and two, if in choosing one, one and one and one and so and as soon and as so much. To double it was not so difficult. After that, and not nearly after that. Ask after it to ask after it.

Picasso and to ask after it.

Further and farther and farther and further. And further.

Once in a way and indicated. It was indicated to me that there was no difference between there was no difference in between there was all the difference between there was that difference and in between and in between and there was that difference. In between and there was that difference. What is the difference between inauguration and inaugurated. Markedly. What is the difference markedly what is markedly the difference between inauguration and inaugurated.

More in the meantime more and in the meantime.

Next.

Not next.

And so next.

When they went away and say and say that they went away.

And not next.

And as next.

And as next and as they went away and say and say and as they went away and as next.

Next next they went away and say and say and they went away and next next. And next and they went away and say.

This is ready and there and there and this and this and this is ready and there. And there and this is ready and there and this and this is ready and there.

If in a minute four in a minute two in a minute too in a minute for in a minute if in a minute. In a minute.

Fairly if he doubted fairly if he doubted, fairly if he doubted at a time like this, fairly if he doubted very fairly if he doubted very fairly if he doubted at a time like this.

Like this moreover.

After that what changes what changes after that, after that what changes and what changes after that and after that and what changes and after that and what changes after that.

Niece and nephew nearly niece and nephew nearly and as nearly and not as nephew and not as niece and not as niece and nephew next.

Only, on that and only only with that, beginning only beginning with that, they come there comes, only beginning with that, there only comes, as there comes as they come only coming as only coming for that and as only coming for that.

To change more to change more to change to change to change more, to change more to exchange more and coming out of that and only coming out of that.

Coming out of that, come out of that coming out of that. And now to bow. How do do you do how do you do and forgive you everything and there is nothing to forgive.

Pablo as a name.

Georges as a name.

Juan as a name.

André as a name.

Pablo Georges Juan André as a name. Pablo Georges Juan as a name Pablo Georges as a name Pablo as a name.

Pablo Georges Juan as a name.

Pablo Georges Juan André as a name.
A long interval as a name.
An interval as a name.
As an interval as a name.
And then a reason.
And then a reason oh as oh as then a reason.
As then a reason.
The reason is.
As then a reason and the reason is.
To let us then and a reason.
As a reason and to let us then. And a reason.
He came first.
And a reason.
They came first.
And a reason.
They came at first.
And the reason.
He came at first.
And for this reason.
He came at first they came at first they came first he came first
and for a reason.
Now kindly might. They now might. He now might. He now
might and for a reason.
At first.
If to feel it at first, if they feel it at first, if they feel it at first if
he feels it first, if he feels it first, if at first, if first, if first and if at
first. If at first and if at first. If at first and feel it and feel it first
and at first.
In this way rejected addresses, rejected dresses rejected and
dresses rejected and addresses rejected addresses rejected and ad-
dresses rejected and dresses. Does this bring just as many mem-
ories bring back just as many bring back just as many and just as
many and bring back.
And so many as are suited. And as many as are suited.
To give a list.
First list.
As a list.
This is as a list and this list and this list is this list.
The list.
First. All of it.
Second. All and all of it.
Third. All of it and all of it.

Fourth. All of it and so and so and all of it.

Fifth. Eradically and so forth and all and all of it.

Fourth fifth and sixth. The lists follow.

The history, history, the history, and history, the history of it, and and so much and as much, this is as much as the this is as much as the history of it and the last, the last was the five and the last was that the five if five are sitting at a table and one of them is leaning on it and at last four and if four are sitting at a table and one of them is leaning on it and at last four. So four so forth.

And so forth.

The history of it is this. We can carefully, we can, we can and as carefully and we can. The history of it is this it is not only prepared but it is also undertaken. We undertake to we do undertake to we have undertaken to we have not and we have not at all and we haven't at all undertaken to do that and that and this and so forth.

The history of it is this. Once upon a time there was born a little girl. A little boy had been born three years before. This gave them both this interest. And then as to weaning. In replying to this authoritatively there was interruption. Often and again and in no circumstances was there any reception. How many must be present to make a reception.

This history of it is this, this is the history of it.

Is pleasant prize pleasant, the prize is pleasant, is as pleasant, she is as pleasant, a prize is pleasant. She is a prize and she is pleasant.

This is what happened for a reason.

Among the influences that have made me what I am.

I am told.

The first thing that is to be noticed is grey and green. The next thing to be noticed is green and blue, the next thing to be noticed is blue and brown, the next thing to be noticed is brown and black and the next thing to be noticed is black and red. So much to notice. So much notice. To notice so much.

After that very likely.

When and men when and mended, when and men when, when then, author and authority for instance.

He said there was no instance of further development when rapidly fortunately arbitrarily and as an accidental accusation. He further said that for most for almost, almost all planned almost all plans, he furthermore said that if cherries are so, that if cherries are so, he furthermore said and he furthermore said it. So many thousands so many thousands and more.

Finally the thing that impressed me most was this, and fortunately at first, fairly at first, finally the thing that impressed me most was this.

It was an advantage it was more than that it was as an advantage that it was considered, considerably an advantage.

For instance when an antagonism to the generosity of all the rest was shown, more or less or less more or less.

Antedated. Antedated and antedated.

The development was happily atoned for and accounted for it was an account of partial familiarity.

Furthermore useless it was furthermore as useless as ever to fasten it as carelessly as that. As much so.

When the fact was understood when this factor became known enthusiasm gradually continued. In my way and it is in my way. So differently urged urged to go away and so as a conclusion.

To come to a conclusion. Agreements agreements agreements, add to agreements. Disagreements and not to add minerals. This caused this was caused this was partially the cause and this was partially and because and because this was partially concurred in.

When for fourteen years older when for or fourteen years older how old are they when they stand up sit down and walk around. We did.

Next.

To-day it was very curious but we felt no surprise whatever when we were intrusted with the welfare of him of her of them of those who can be seen to be not nearly as often duplicated as formerly. And very fairly, very fairly fairly and very, not at all an indiscretion.

As I was saying when she was born it was as nicely as ever.

As I was saying when he was prepared as relatively speaking it was in no sense an absolute denial of authenticity. No indeed carelessness and inevitably there would come an interval. Indeed one may say so.

This leads to that.

Afterwards and a whole ship afterwards and wholly and a ship afterwards what ship.

A ship.

Afterwards and what ship a ship.

Piles and pile driving. Pile-driving, piles of pile driving and afterwards a ship. Shipping afterwards shipping, shipping it afterwards. Piles and pile-driving and shipping it afterwards.

A ship not a ship, not a ship at sea. When this you see remember me.

137

All of it makes no more of it, more of it makes no more than more than all of it.

Friendly as friendly.

In that place in the place of it, this is there in place of it and as if it were not so much trouble and if it were not as much trouble as that. If it were as much trouble as that. If it were as much trouble.

All of it all of it for all of it, for all of it as a request. I request you a request for all of it has been refused. A refusal for all of it has been requested. And after that there had been an instance of agreement, you agree I agree we agree they agree, agreable, agreably. And so forth. Fortunately.

As every one and they see and they saw, as every one and they saw as every one and they see. As every one and they see. I see the moon and the moon sees me. They see and I see. Seasonably.

As if an extra, it was as if it it was an extra.

An extra and an extra. Where is there an extra. When there is an extra then there is an extra there. There is an extra here. Here is the extra.

As much as that. There is an extra here as much as that. As much as that. There is an extra and as much as that and here. And so forth. Special extra. A special extra, as much as that. A special extra as much as that and so forth. We know the reason why and he said all of it Sunday. Sunday is especially so, some day is especially so. And so forth.

ADDENDUM.

To be added to by this and that Paul is all.
Or Paul is all.

1924

138

DESCRIPTIONS OF LITERATURE

A book which shows that the next and best is to be found out when there is pleasure in the reason.

For this reason.

A book in which by nearly all of it finally and an obstruction it is planned as unified and nearly a distinction. To be distinguished is what is desired.

A book where in part there is a description of their attitude and their wishes and their ways.

A book which settles more nearly than has ever been yet done the advantages of following later where they have found that they must go.

A book where nearly everything is prepared.

A book which shows that as it is nearly equally best to say so, as they say and say so.

A book which makes a mention of all the times that even they recognize as important.

A book which following the story the story shows that persons incurring blame and praise make no return for hospitality.

A book which admits that all that has been found to be looked for is of importance to places.

A book which manages to impress it upon the young that those who oppose them follow them and follow them.

A book [which] naturally explains what has been the result of investigation.

A book that marks the manner in which longer and shorter proportionately show measure.

A book which makes no mistake in describing the life of those who can be happy.

The next book to appear is the one in which more emphasis will be given to numbers of them.

A book which when you open it attracts attention by the undoubted denial of photography as an art.

A book which reminds itself that having had a custom it only needs more of it and more.

A book which can not imbue any one with any desire except the one which makes changes come later.

A book explaining why more of them feel as they do.

A book which attracts attention.

A book which is the first book in which some one has been telling why on one side rather than on the other there is a tendency to shorten shorten what. Shorten more.

A book which plans homes for any of them.

A book a book telling why when at once and at once.

A book telling why when [?he] said that, she answered it as if it were the same.

A book which tells why colonies have nearly as many uses as they are to have now.

A book which makes no difference between one jeweler and another.

A book which mentions all the people who have had individual chances to come again.

A book in translation about eggs and butter.

A book which has great pleasure in describing whether any further attention is to be given to homes where homes have to be homes.

A book has been carefully prepared altogether.

A book and deposited as well.

A book describing fishing exactly.

A book describing six and six and six.

A book describing six and six and six seventy-two.

A book describing Edith and Mary and flavouring fire.

A book describing as a man all of the same ages all of the same ages and nearly the same.

A book describing hesitation as exemplified in plenty of ways.

A book which chances to be the one universally described as energetic.

A book which makes no mistakes either in description or in departure or in further arrangements.

A book which has made all who read it think of the hope they have that sometime they will have fairly nearly all of it at once.

A book in which there is no complaint made of forest fires and water.

A book more than ever needed.

A book made to order and the only thing that was forgotten in ordering was what no one objects to. Can it easily be understood. It can and will.

A book which places the interest in those situations which have something to do with recollections and with returns.

A book with more respect for all who have to hear and have heard a book with more respect for all who have heard it.

A book more than ever read.

A book by and by.

A book not nearly so much better than ever.

A book and fourteen. The influence of this book is such that no one has had more than this opportunity.

A book of dates and fears.

A book more than ever a description of happiness and as you were.

A book which makes the end come just as soon as it is intended.

A book which asks questions of every one.

A book fairly certain of having admirers when at once there are admirers of it.

A book which shows that agreeableness can be a feature of it all.

A book which makes a play of daughter and daughters.

A book which has character and shows that no one need deceive themselves as to the sending of gifts.

A book which has a description of the selection and placing of chairs as an element in Viennese and American life.

A book which standardizes requests and announcements.

A book which urges and reasonably so the attraction of some for others.

A book in which there is no mention of advantages.

A book attaching importance to english and french names.

A book which has to be carefully read in order to be understood and so that the illusion of summer and summer and summer and summer does not remain deceiving. So much so.

A book narrowly placed on the shelf and often added. Added to that.

A book of addresses invented for the sake of themselves.

A book and a bookstore. A book for them. Will they be in it.

1924

FIVE WORDS IN A LINE

Five words in a line.
Bay and pay make a lake.
Have to be held with what.
They have to be held with what they have to be held.
Dependent of dependent of why.
With a little cry.
Make of awake.
Five words in a line.
Four words in a line.
They make it with it being please to have withheld with with it.
Four words in one line.
If to pay by postage.
At all to delay to pay by postage.
If he is he then he will follow me but will he. With them. With
will he.
Really. Five words in a line.
There is every way to-day to say in with a whitened end with it.
Pardon there with ours.
It is very little that will. That in that in that will.
Four words in one line.
Have withhold. Have withheld.
Six words in one line.
They were alike. With them. They went with wish. If they had
the possibility of annoyance.
Six words in one line.
They are as well as alike.
Three were by theirs allied.
If they were true to usual. A refusal. Made carriage with a weed-
ing. Without varied vary roses.
But with them.
Withhold.

They look at him and they know what he thinks.
Now they could when they look at him.

When they were married by him this made away.

Barred to be barred.
Why little a long a lain made with a piled with adapt.

Very benevolently she left for him.

If she could with and did dazzle.

Why were they changing two in yet or all day.

It is very happily that it is with added that it is as it is a gold or
is told.

Commence again that we like waving.

Once every day once a day they make it do. By this time a part
of it is impressed favorably with keeping. If not by and with al-
lowance. They mean that if they know.

What does it look like if it looks like it.

They came to the country and they asked them not to and they
did a little at a time with whom with flourishes.

JENNY SOLOMON

Matter pan has acuteness in return she said with they did.

Only now nearly known names a press with them.

A SOFA

Married a presently for them and known. It might be larger.

It might not be as high as with them.
To come back.
If it looks like it.
Without it.
With it.
If it looks like it with it.
Four words in each line.
If it does it looks as it does it looks like it.
Does look like it.
It does look like it.
Five words in a line is right.
By never being suspicious and always being careful she has
never been robbed. ○

1929

VI

Syntax and Elucidation

From 1928 to 1931 Gertrude Stein was preoccupied with the exploration of grammar and its relation to writing in-the-present, with poetry and its relation to prose in a non-Aristotelian world, with narration in-the-present as differentiated from narrative, and with the writing of history as an in-the-present process.

Key books written at this time which show these concerns were How to Write *(1931),* Before the Flowers of Friendship Faded Friendship Faded *(1930) and* Stanzas in Meditation *(1932), as well as* The Autobiography of Alice B. Toklas *(1932).*

By the end of this period, and certainly after the publication of The Autobiography, *Gertrude Stein had passed from being a rather private, specialized writer to being a public personality with a large reading audience. She began to differentiate two kinds of writing: (1) "identity" writing—done for her new reading audience and intended to be popularly understood (2) "entity" writing—done for her own creative purposes and with no sense of audience.*

The first pieces in this section were still written as essentially private works. With "Thoughts on American Contemporary Feeling" the audience is anticipated. With "Reflection on the Atomic Bomb," Gertrude Stein's last written work, we have essentially an audience piece.

Volume II of this present work, How Writing Is Written, *will trace the complexities of this later development in more detail.*

"We Came. A History" poses the problem of history as now. *Everything which happens in the moment is seen as equally historical. Even the structure of the sentences is shot through with equal signs. They disturb the traditional syntax and seem to imply that whatever is on either side of them has equal weight, or absolute equality. Gertrude Stein had always been interested in Cezanne's composition and his way of keeping the "values even" on the surface of his canvasses. She had "discovered" that Walt Whitman's title* Leaves of Grass *meant that every leaf of grass was as important as every other leaf of grass. Now she keeps her values even in writing history by describing only what happens in the present*

146

moment, and by dappling the surface of her prose with phrases, clauses and sentences resembling a Cezannesque balance.

"Evidence" is a study in the internal balance of sentences. Gertrude Stein once wrote that writing must go up and down like an old fashioned weighing machine. Here she balances sight, sound, sense and syntax. She thought the closing sentence of this work was very nearly perfect: "Once when they were nearly ready they had ordered it to close."

"Left to Right" is a study in narration—telling something without telling a story, telling the excitement, structure, dynamics of an event. Balancing out the emotion. Making sentences and paragraphs that do their work.

"Thoughts on an American Contemporary Feeling" is a meditation on the difference between the creative artist and the professional "explainer"—the aesthetician, the critic and the teacher. Gertrude Stein locates the creative artist as neither ahead of his time nor behind it but "with it," being sensitively aware of it in the moment of creation, being his own contemporary. She locates the "explainer" as necessarily behind his time, for he necessarily deals with ideas which have already been formulated and are therefore already dead. For her the vitality was always in the "now" moment. This piece anticipates Gertrude Stein's desire to write for an audience, which culminated in the two autobiographies, Lectures in America (1934), Narration (1935) and other "popular" books of the last decade of her life.

"Reflection on the Atomic Bomb," Gertrude Stein's last written work, is a final meditation, halfway intended for a popular audience. At a time when the atomic bomb was a world concern, she rejected the preoccupation with fear and destruction and instead accepted only the living, the natural and the common-sensical as worthy of attention. Such had always been both her personal and creative position.

WE CAME. A HISTORY

A History

We came and were pleased with what we saw. It was very much as pleasant as it could be. It was nearly with which we were to be as much as possible contented. In no time we were made where we were.

This is an introduction to residing.

A nephew of an old woman could be shot having been mistaken for a wild boar not by those who had the right to destroy the animal by themselves but by those who were doing it illegally. So then they made it be as if he had been killed. The result of which is that we have no wild hare.

One day we had two visitors they stayed not with us but in the neighborhood two days and during that time they were with us and we found it agreeable to show them things that were known. What is known homes and places and lakes and churches.

An attitude of being made agreeable to those who do not care to address him. What is history. Believe them it is not for their pleasure that they do it. History is this anything that they say and that they do and anything that is made for them by them such as not speaking to them in case that he is turned away from them. This is historical. What did they do. They were willing to like them and to tell it of them in telling everything.

What is historical. Sentences are historical. They will not encourage children. This is not historical. They will be made very dependent on men and women. This might be historical. He was very much pleased with the hope of release. This is historical. What happened. He resigned himself to remaining where he was and in this way he neither endeared himself nor made them relieve him when he was willing. This is history because it is accompanied by reluctance. Reluctance is not necessarily history nor is decision.

I like white because dahlias are beautiful in color. Tube roses come from onions, in every sense of the word and the way of saying it is attractive to her.

How do you like what you have heard.=History must be distinguished=From mistakes.=History must not be what is=Happening.=History must not be about=Dogs and balls in all=The meaning of those=Words history must be=Something unusual and =Nevertheless famous and=Successful. History must=Be the occasion of having=In every way established a=Precedent history must=Be all there is of importance=In their way successively= History must be an open=Reason for needing them=There which it is as they=Are perfectly without a=Doubt that it is interested.= History cannot be an accident.=They make history they=Are in the place of it.=II=History leaves no place=For which they ask will =They be made more of=In case of the disaster=Which has not overtaken=Any one. Historically there=Is no disaster because= Those who make history=Cannot be overtaken=As they will make =History which they do=Because it is necessary=That every one will=Begin to know that=They must know that=History is what it is=Which it is as they do=Know that history is not=Just what every one=Does who comes and=Prefers days to more=Than ever which they have=History must again be=Caught and taught and =Not be that it is tiring=To play with balls.=It is not tiring to go on=And make the needle=Which goes in and out=Be careful not at all=History is made by a very=Few who are important= And history is what that=One says. History is=This it is the neck- lace=Which makes pansies=Be made well of stones=Which they are likely=To be. This is not=History history is made=By them they make history.=III=One who was remarkable=Addressed them as follows.=Come when you like and=Leave when you like =And send what you like=And play what you like=But and in this there=Can be no mistake=Do not care more for=Nasturtiums than for=Tube roses. It was a=Moment the moment=When there was certainty=That it was that and by=Itself they were told= That it was not different.=There are three things=That are histor- ical.=Tube roses heliotrope and lavender.=There may be fragrant lilies=And other delights but=History is made and=Preserved by heliotrope=Lavender and tube-roses.=History is made and re- mains=A delight by reason=Of certainty and certainty=Depends upon a result=Achieved directly by a=Surprise not a surprise =In fact nor in thought=Nor in result but a=Surprise in the de- light=And the delight is not=A surprise the surprise=Is in con- firmation and so=It is undoubtedly real=That history is made= By accomplishment=And accomplishment is=A surprise which it is=So that there is not=A possibility of coming=And going his- torically.=This will be understood=Readily not by them.=Nor by me for them=Nor is it without doubt=That they are as for them =In elegance. In order=Not to end and finish=They will say it has=Not happened but it has.=With them in time.=The time for tasting is=Also as you may say=They have forgotten that=It is not worth while=This has to do with grapes=And barley and wheat=And also meat and rice=And also ducks and birds=And also hens and cats=And eggs. All this has=Been a history of pleasantness=In arrangement which=They made when they= Were pleased.=IV=But in duration they might=With which they please days=More just as willing pass=In neglect receive on loan =It is call of=They will be willingly here=Not as if alright lain =Made it a forgotten thing=That she could thank layers=Not without use of it=Partly as when known mind=They mind whether they do=A well which it is=Counting from this of it=In much of it owned.=Likeness makes places be where=They must have what now=Come to smoulder with our=Nearly formed alike with moist =Allowed which is in his=To make those carry here=She sleeps but is annoyed=And so she mentions them=That is arranged like it=A part of which cut=You know how like it=Known how you like it.=V=But as will which is of it=Nearly come back to help exploit it=They might in the meantime see which=In a way it is a choice=By the time that it is finished=They must have whatever they will like=It is very dangerous to help it=As they mean to hold all there=As they very well happen with it=To hope to have it like it.=VI=Please save them=For little things=In a million=They make which=It is vastly=Nor more than=As left nearly=In a tree=Which came like=A better parasol=Made into two=The like of which=Is not felt=By those who=In the meanwhile=Are better inclined=Than they were=As much as=In silently waking.=As she named.=All of it=Is made there=In quietly=Second to none=In recollection barely=Hours at a time= They will share=What they have=With those known=By their name=They will hear=What they do=In woods alike=And rhododendrons hortensias=And peppers alike=They will have=More of it=Chain of vines=Made of morning-glories=Which are renowned=And blushing pails=Which made treasure=Be happily theirs=Oh leave it=With them here=Because as a matter of fact =They will be better off.=VII=Touch butter but not flower= Whether either or for another=Make hopes leave it all=Never bother them with it=As very likely they will=She knows how to refuse=Leave it for them there=They will have a use=For it as an almanac=In splendid weather=Which they expect=VIII=Bother me with that=But it is part of it=In that case do not leave it=But it is of no use to me=Why do they not like it.=Do not say they when you mean them=They like it very well=They will use it for themselves=Once in a while they will not know what to do with it.=It is the only reason for it not being made better. =The change from all of it is well enough.=They have it=As they like=Which they regulate.=IX=Acrobacy fools them.=X=Just when they went=They knew as well=As if it was=Their wish to go=In which in case=They were as often=Left alone with it= As it might be=Too much coming there=Without its being said= Jackets are necessary here=In a little while=Very often a veil= Is what they know=When they hear it=In the meanwhile too= It is actually read=By the time only=In case of separation=Two have to order=All that they need=May be she will=But in and about=It is not likely=Which she means.=XI=Autobiography ought to=Have made doors=They will scare them=XII=By their help=It is usual=To succeed nicely=Without their help=Which they give=As it is=Ought to go=They must and=Will have what-ever=They want here=By the time=They are willing=To allow banking=Which have helped them.=XIII=It is easy to see that they move differently=XIV=I called it audience and then frame or form but the question is not that it is not composition it is not that it is beginning and middle and ending without that anybody can end and begin and the middle is easier than anything.=XV=I am not busy=When he is neglected=This is not often=Because she is there=XVI=Ours are made for them=They will ask for it =They need two rests for it=Because it is helped more than they like by it=Because in searching for doves=Doves are named pig-eons by butter.=Do not be blamed for failure=Ask them are they ready=But is it wise to=Because it may annoy them=Press them to remain here=They will like it if they stay=Little by little it will help=Not to be restless like that=He wants his dinner=After it is over he will be=Just as restless=This is why they never pay any attention to what he does.=They must call him anyway.=XVII=I do not think it would do=To bathe him on a Sunday=This is the reason=It is easy to be quiet=And to give it as a reason=For com-ing to-day=Florence is made to George=Now listen to that.=It does surprise you=Florence is not yet married to George but they have had the dinner of betrothal which was later than noon and a good deal of bother.=The first of September Florence is to be married to George.=XVIII=Any one believes that things equal to the same thing are equal to each other. Any little way that is like a pleasure.=Just why they came=Is the same way=In which they waited=In liking having bought it=Which made them go=They went away at once.=XIX=It is easy to keep count.=One two three all out but she.=It is easy to keep count and make a mistake.=

Slenderness keeps them busy.=Ought they to be busy=With it=
Anything artificial is an annoyance example artificial silk.=All
history is cautious.

1930

EVIDENCE

EVIDENCE

They come and go. It is the cruelest thing I ever heard is the favorite phrase of Gilbert. And he is right. He has heard many cruel things and it is the cruelest thing that he has heard.

EVIDENCE

A lady sitting and working at tapestry which although it is of to-day in design and color looks ancient. The bell rings and two friends come in they ask may we tell you about it. I have taken the measures but you can measure it yourself. The one who replies is a friend of the other one who has not been in before. They may call each other friends although the one is tired of his mother.

EVIDENCE

Portrait of Bravig Imbs

May Sage has a page who does her errands. He may have dreamed and now to his mother he says see and she knows where they were by their help. If any one is well they make it do.

How do you do is easily said.

He waited.

An old fashioned short story.

EVIDENCE

Cater will be with them as with him.

A sentence is annoyed when they mention believe it is not for pleasure that I do it. I was just going on and that dog stopped. Part of it is explained.

How are eggs made of butter.

If they eat.

Eggs and butter.

If they eat eggs and butter.

These are good examples of sentences.

EVIDENCE

We think that the last time is the worst.

A sentence has had they wish. They wish for this and they get it. There is no mistake about it. Once when they went away they were equal to being estranged once when they were very well. It is best to be always prepared for the weather to have fur coats in winter and light clothes in summer.

Once when they were very agreeable they were settled in the place which they had hoped to have. It is more than occasional with absolute and about. It is not what they think that they feel without it being made easier. They are like which they need for their business. They must be softer than their thoughts. With them they please them. They will be well enough known to be stared at when they should know everything themselves.

This is the meeting. They will have plates with them when they go where they will have best and most now or there.

To come to the subject that they had better have fur coats in winter and lighter clothes in summer.

It is useless to be hurt by their disappointment not in a dream but in their thoughts.

They will color or allow might and pleases.

It is very good to have welcomes when they are here. He could be the son and the better have changed when they were daunted. It is close to them.

Think of a subject. How are every half hour known not as halves not even as half of an hour but thirty minutes. It is signed they went away.

Every thirty minutes we need a lead. They and all of it is an invidious distinction. Silence and settlement have help for them.

It is when he is breathless that he asks who can compare me to a Russian. They will not have half an hour to themselves.

All are lonely when they print are there clothes. They must have it in case of their dispersal.

Canning to be canning can be in two senses. They can think and they can be a fairly loaned to them. You must never start one to be different.

That is an error in regular arrangement and they changed soaps.

Now then wandering is a thing.

They will educate one with another as of one.

Fortunately it is better to smell china lilies than ivy because ivy can be in miniature.

Once when they were nearly ready they had ordered it to close.

1930

LEFT TO RIGHT

Arthur William came to see me while I was in the country. He proposed to me that we should have a book together. This was not really true; he had done his and I had done mine. We both had seen the others.

I accepted all that he proposed. The book was to be illustrated by drawings by people we both knew. He had made the selection. I made an addition but we accepted everything which was to have all those whom he had selected. Among them was one I did not much care to have as a principal one but it did not make any difference. All the arrangements had been made and I agreed to everything and even sent postals with him to every one, and this was not really an annoyance and it should not have been done.

When I came back from the country it was about a month later I saw everyone, I did not really like anyone they did not like anybody either. But I did not pay much attention because we were all home from the country and every one saw every one and we talked about everybody but when I saw the editor and I did see her I did not say anything about anything but America. This was because everything had already been arranged and there was an exhibition of all the drawings that were being used as illustration for the book that was to appear very soon.

One evening we were all going to a circus to see a man do some marvelous giant swinging. Arthur brought with him the announcements for our book and I did not notice anything. The next morning I looked and it said it was his book and it did not say it was my book and I did not say anything.

I wrote to him and said not at all it must be half mine or something. He said nothing. Then he wrote and said that the way he had decided was the right way and therefore it was too late to change something. Then I went to the editor and said it was necessary to change something. She said why yes of course that is what I think. Just then she was called by someone to come to the telephone. She came back and said that he had said to her he would not let them change anything. I said all right there is nothing to do I am not allowing them to have anything. And that was the way the thing was then.

Now what was happening.

155

Generale Erving was a writer, that is to say he had written not writing but something. That is to say we were writing we were writers who were writing. We were both very fond of him. He was never interfering but he knew everything and he always said something. I knew what he said and I noticed everything. I never noticed that he said a thing. And so it went on. He had been for some time not liking Arthur William. That is to say he had not for some time said anything about liking me or anything.

When Arthur William heard from the editor that I was not giving anything he was furious and said he had asked everyone about everything and he would go on as he had done. I did not ask anyone anything and I wrote to him that I would not give anyone anything unless it was going to be done as I wanted it done. And so we went on.

Then I went to the editor to say I was through with everything. While I was sitting talking we saw someone coming. Arthur William was coming with someone. He came in alone. He was pale, but not trembling. I was not pale but I was trembling. He came up to me and said how do you do. I looked at his hand, and did not say anything. He stopped and began trembling. I sat and waited a little while, and said now this is all of this thing. And I left, and he remained doing something.

I heard about everybody talking. I did see some of them. All of them were interesting. I was talking about everything to everyone. And we never said anything about not repeating what everyone was saying. Everyone said the same thing about everyone and I knew what they said about this thing. I never met Arthur William, and he was talking to everyone and about this thing. And I was talking to everyone about this thing and everyone was talking to me about him and about everything but none of them had anything to say except that everyone said everything that everyone was saying about him, about me and about this thing. And so this was until very much later about a week later one evening.

Generale Erving called me one afternoon on the telephone to tell me something. I said I knew all about Frederick Harvard. Frederick Harvard is a writer who has written and everybody knows all about this thing. Would he be writing something now. Yes he would and he just had and for Arthur William it was very interesting. He was seeing Frederick Harvard and Frederick Harvard called him Arthur but that was nothing everybody called Arthur Arthur but Arthur was calling Frederick Harvard Frederick and that was because Frederick Harvard was going to be writing something that Arthur would be coming to find interesting. I told Generale Erving I knew all about that anybody could have seen that coming.

Generale Erving told me over the telephone that he wanted to fix up everything. It was all right but it would be all right and Arthur was not at all there but he Generale Erving would see him was I willing. Yes I was willing but not so willing that I was willing to be refusing anything before I said it. I was not giving and refusing anything. I was willing. Yes. Yes said Generale I understand.

Of course you do I said but let us repeat it. Are you coming or are you going I am not doing anything. I will see you to-morrow evening. Well you do not want to forget that I am here only to be accommodating. I do not need anything and it has to be said just like that or nothing. I understand said Generale Erving. I am seeing you tomorrow evening.

Everybody was quiet in between.

Generale Erving came and we spent a pleasant evening. We talked about everything.

He told me some things that Arthur had said that I did not know he said but he did say them. He told about how long Arthur had been saying he had been thinking that he had better do what he was doing. I said I had heard that Arthur was like that from someone who long ago had had enough of him and I said that I was through with him and this was after Generale said that Arthur was ready to say that he was ready to ask me to have him give in. Generale had had a piece of paper on which Arthur had written this thing. When Generale was leaving I gave the paper back to him.

The next day I did nothing. And then there was another week and then I had a letter from Arthur asking me to arrange everything. I did not do anything.

All this time I thought that it was all Arthur William. Perhaps it was and then perhaps I had better not have anything further to do with Generale Erving. Perhaps not. Perhaps I might think over everything. Perhaps I might remember everything. Perhaps Generale would come again and I would see him and I would not say anything. Perhaps he was worried about everything. Perhaps Generale would come again and I would tell him I was busy and could not see him.

I went somewhere and there I saw Frederick Harvard. He did not want to see me. I had never known him. I went up to him and I said to him I hope you are all well. And he was nervous and he said, yes, I am all well. And your wife I said to him I hope she is quite well again and he said yes she was quite well again.

When I had waited a little longer I said to the editor that I was not giving her anything and so Arthur did not have anything and that was all over. I did however have something and I kept everything and I can use everything. I sent a card to Generale Erving and I said I did not want to have any further acquaintance with him.

And now before I go out I always look up and down to see that none of them are coming. We were after that never friends or anything. This is all this true story and it was exciting.

1931

THOUGHTS ON AN AMERICAN
CONTEMPORARY FEELING

And they were right. But. Is it contemporary. May be it is but I doubt it. May I quote myself. "For this reason as in quoting Lord Grey it is quite certain that nations not actively threatened are at least several generations behind themselves militarily so æsthetically they are more than several generations behind themselves and it is very much too bad, it is so much very much more exciting and satisfactory for everybody if one can have contemporaries if all one's contemporaries could be one's contemporaries." "By this I mean all this."

When they meant what they said and they said it not those who had said it, but these said it, that America to be American that Americans to be American should be concerned about America and Americans and should be concerned about Americans and America by being in America. When these said it I did not think they meant it when they said it. And they do. And the reason of it. Is this.

America that is the United States of America and it is very interesting was throughout the nineteenth century beginning living that is to say they were beginning living being made out of the eighteenth century they were beginning in the nineteenth century that is in all the nineteenth century they were beginning living beginning and living in the twentieth century. And now what are they to do. Having done something they must be. Looking backward. That is. Natural enough.

And how do you look backward. By looking forward. And what do they see. As they look forward. They see what they had to do before they could look backward. And there we have it all.

And now to make it all clearer. Those who are saying that they should stay at home mean that as America has done something that is as it has created the twentieth century and we who were and are Americans have all through the nineteenth century created the twentieth century for all who are in the twentieth century, those who concern themselves with things æsthetic being as I say when I quote myself inevitably several generations behind their generation think quite reasonably that what has been done is to do. But it has been done, and the generation living as contemporaries they on the contrary are occupying themselves to continue America by being outside of America. And so as usual æsthetically those who concern themselves with what they consider the most contemporary of art and literature are many generations behind themselves.

To make it all clearer. The after civil war congressmen when they said that America should make Americans in America were alright, and Americans were being made in America, but soon America was and now is made and Americans are Americans the people who solemnly concern themselves with æsthetic things think that it makes a difference where Americans are. Of course it does not. Americans having been made. And they are made. On the contrary the congressmen know now that Americans being Americans America having been made and having made the twentieth century, Americans can be wherever they are and they make arrangements accordingly. It is only those who concern themselves with æsthetic things critically and academically being several generations behind themselves can really believe when they think these things.

1931

REFLECTION ON THE ATOMIC BOMB

They asked me what I thought of the atomic bomb. I said I had not been able to take any interest in it.

I like to read detective and mystery stories, I never get enough of them but whenever one of them is or was about death rays and atomic bombs I never could read them. What is the use, if they are really as destructive as all that there is nothing left and if there is nothing there nobody to be interested and nothing to be interested about. If they are not as destructive as all that then they are just a little more or less destructive than other things and that means that in spite of all destruction there are always lots left on this earth to be interested or to be willing and the thing that destroys is just one of the things that concerns the people inventing it or the people starting it off, but really nobody else can do anything about it so you have to just live along like always, so you see the atomic [bomb] is not at all interesting, not any more interesting than any other machine, and machines are only interesting in being invented or in what they do, so why be interested. I never could take any interest in the atomic bomb, I just couldn't any more than in everybody's secret weapon. That it has to be secret makes it dull and meaningless. Sure it will destroy a lot and kill a lot, but it's the living that are interesting not the way of killing them, because if there were not a lot left living how could there be any interest in destruction. Alright, that is the way I feel about it. And really way down that is the way everybody feels about it. They think they are interested about the atomic bomb but they really are not not any more than I am. Really not. They may be a little scared, I am not so scared, there is so much to be scared of so what is the use of bothering to be scared, and if you are not scared the atomic bomb is not interesting.

Everybody gets so much information all day long that they lose their common sense. They listen so much that they forget to be natural. This is a nice story.

1946

SOURCES AND ACKNOWLEDGEMENTS

The texts as printed in this book follow the published texts (including variations between British and American spelling) except for obvious printer's errors.

Thanks are hereby given to Robert A. Wilson and to Gunnar F. Gustin, Jr. who were kind enough to supply copies of certain of these texts from their Gertrude Stein collections; and to Donald Gallup, Yale University Library, who has kindly made the balance of the sources readily available. Particular thanks should also go to Mr. Calman A. Levin (of Daniel C. Joseph, Literary Executor of the Gertrude Stein Estate) for his unfailing help and encouragement in this project, and to Seamus Cooney of Western Michigan University who tirelessly proofread the book against the original printed sources.

First appearances of the material in this volume were as follows: "Wear," *Broom*, January 1923; "How Could They Marry Her," *Envoy*, January 1951; "Water Pipe," *larus*, February 1927; "Relief Work in France," *Life*, December 27, 1917; "The Great American Army," *Vanity Fair*, June 1918; "One Has Not Lost One's Marguerite," *Black and Blue Jay*, April 1926; "J. R. I," *Vanity Fair*, March 1919; "J. R. II," *Vanity Fair*, March 1919; "The Meaning of the Bird," *Vanity Fair*, March 1919; "A Deserter," *Vanity Fair*, March 1919; "Mrs. Thursby," *Soil*, December 1916; "Mrs. Emerson," *Close up*, August 1927; "J. H. Jane Heap," *Little Review*, May 1929; "Indian Boy," *The Reviewer*, January 1924; "A Stitch in time saves nine," *Ex Libris*, March 1925; "Troubadour," *Ex Libris*, June 1925; "Oscar Wilde Discovers America," *Chicago Daily Tribune*, August 8, 1936; "Sir Francis Rose," Wildenstein Gallery, 1934; "Sir Francis Rose," *The Arts Club*, Chicago, 1934; "Stieglitz," (in) *America and Alfred Stieglitz*, 1934; "Picabia," *Valentine Gallery*, N.Y., 1934; "Elie Lascaux," *The Arts Club*, Chicago, 1936; "Sir Francis Rose," *The Mayor Gallery*, London, 1939; "Sherwood's Sweetness," *Story*, September/October 1941; "From Dark to Day," *Vogue, London*, November 1945; "Raoul Dufy," *Harper's Bazaar*, December 1949; "Vacation in Brittany," *Little Review*, Spring 1922; "Ireland," *Der Quersch-*

163

nitt, March 1925; "Dinner," *The Banyan Press,* December 1948; "Readings," *Banyan Press,* Pawlet, Vermont, 1947; "Today We Have a Vacation," *The Banyan Press,* December 1948; "Mildred's Thoughts" (in) *American Caravan,* 1927; "If He Thinks," *Transition,* January 1928; "Procession," *Programme,* June 1935; Daniel Webster," *New Directions,* 1937; "Lucretia Borgia," *Creative Writing,* 1938; "Studies in Conversation," *Transition,* September 1927; "Are There Arithmetics," *Oxford 1927,* May 28, 1927; "Made a Mile Away," *Transition,* November 1927; "Descriptions of Literature," *Transition,* Summer 1928; "Five Words in a Line," *Pagany,* Winter 1930; "We Came. A History," (in) *Readies For Bob Brown's Machine,* 1931; "Evidence," (in) *Modern Things,* 1934; "Left to Right," *Story,* November 1933; "Thoughts on an American Contemporary Feeling," *Creative Age,* February 1932; "Reflection on the Atomic Bomb," *Yale Poetry Review,* December 1947.

Printed September 1973 in Santa Barbara and Ann Arbor by Noel Young & Edwards Brothers, Inc. Design by Barbara Martin. This edition is published in paper wrappers; there are 750 hardcover copies; & 50 numbered copies handbound in boards by Earle Grey.